JUST LOOK!!

IT HAPPENS MORE THAN YOU THINK

LEARN RED FLAGS AND SAFEGUARDS TO DETECT AND PROTECT YOUR BUSINESS FROM EMPLOYEE FRAUD

JOHN BALL

JOHN BALL
SPEAKER · AUTHOR
MOTIVATOR

COPYRIGHT
IT HAPPENS MORE THAN YOU THINK

Edited by James MacEachern

Printed in Canada

First printing edition, 2023 sept 11-1 JM
isbn: 978-1-7387241-1-6

TABLE OF CONTENTS

THE AUTHOR

The author's name is John Ball. Born in 1967 to parents who immi-
grated from the UK to Canada in 1966.
He left home at 15 years old to pursue musical ambitions and returned

back home when he was 28. He got married and had two children who are now grown and in University. In 1996, with a partner, they opened a recording studio, and it grew into a design and manufacturing company that serviced recording studios, record labels, and bands, and eventually software companies, fortune 500 companies, government agencies, and advertising agencies alike. Making #16 on Profit magazines fastest growing Canadian companies. The company continued to grow over the years, adding book manufacturing and binding as well. However, in 2009 - 2010, the company started to lose money and seem to have issues after issue. Ball and his team could not put their fingers on it.

Just prior to these two years, they had hired a trusted friend to help them run the Administrative Financial and HR areas of the company. A coincidence? I don't think so......

AH-HA MOMENT OR OH-OH MOMENT?

In 2011 , the company had a devastating fire. No one was hurt but they lost everything. Nothing was left, not even a paper clip. Shortly after the fire, the Vice President of the company uncovered a fraud. A fraud that was being perpetrated by the same trusted friend that was hired. John realized that someone was stealing. That was the problem, but the bigger problem was that he didn't look and wasn't looking where he needed to. So obvious…

They spent the next 10 -11 years in courtroom after courtroom.
Running in circles trying to make things right again.
John is determined not to let it define him.

 " If we can turn this around and into something that can really help others. We can turn it from something bad into something that does good. Even if we can prevent one person from going through what we did, it will be worth it."

~

For my Family, friends and colleagues. Thanks to all of you who supported me throughout the years, I know it hasn't been easy. Also, Thank you to everyone that scattered…..
That drives me more than anything else.

~

PREFACE

I have to admit, when I read my Authors Bio, it didn't really sound so bad, but then I remembered why I am doing this.

I have to remind myself to make sure that I convey in a clear and concise manner just how difficult and stressful it can be to navigate employee fraud of the size we experienced.

If I don't convey this as truthfully and real as I can, I would be doing a disservice to the reader. Everyone's experience is different. In cases where the fraudster pleads guilty and expresses remorse, the experience would be very different than ours. We seemed to have all the extras attached; it was like an overview of all the extreme things that could happen during an employee fraud.

The main reason for this book is to try to mitigate and even eliminate employee fraud being perpetrated against a company.

To save employers, their families and friends some of the stress we all endured. Looking back, I can see it all was completely avoidable.

In the two years before the fraud, we literally ran in circles worrying about why we were losing money when I could have just looked. We spent the majority of our time chasing our tails, instead of selling and nurturing clients. What opportunities did we miss? What important time with our families did we miss? I can only look forward and hope this does some good, heals some wounds, and strengthens some bonds.

PUBLIC SPEAKING

The idea of this book was an afterthought. It was never meant to be a standalone book but was essentially going to be a companion to my public speaking. However, I'm hoping it will help for those who cannot attend one of my speaking engagements. That being said, I will always try to make myself available to anyone who has questions or concerns.

WHY I AM WRITING THIS BOOK.

In 2011 the company had a devastating fire. No one was hurt, but we lost everything. Nothing was left, not even a paper clip. Shortly after the fire, we uncovered fraud perpetrated by a trusted employee- one that shook us to the core and took years to deal with.

When I look back, the signs were everywhere; red flags were present, and I wasn't looking.

Initially, I wasn't going to discuss the details or backstory of my fraud at all. I still have no interest in discussing any details.

Without the backstory, however, I found the book lacked context.

The more I started to write, the more I realized it was necessary to have some of the actual events described so the reader can get a sense of the impact involved. I have also asked former colleagues if they would like to recall in their own perspective what happened and how it affected them. I need the reader to understand the affect this type of crime and the time spent in the legal system has on families, businesses, relationships, and health.

The title of this book was going to be "It Happens More Than You Think". We realized during the editing process that I was saying the phrase "Just Look" at every turn. It's really that simple.

Every time someone asks me advice or about my experience, I would say to them "you know, it happens more than you think". The more I researched and the more people I spoke to made me realize just how true that is.

I hope this helps someone, I really do, but the bottom line is the only way to not be effected by this type of crime is to prevent it from happening at all because if you get caught in the legal aspects of an employee based fraud, there is no way out.

INTRODUCTION

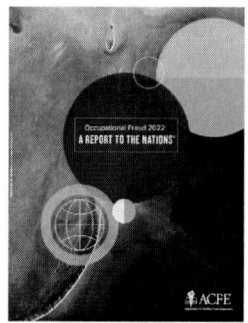

Before we go any further, I think this is the perfect time to introduce an organization called the Association of Certified Fraud Examiners (ACFE) and their annual Report to the Nations. This is where all of the data comes from that I use in my presentations and in the book that accompanies it.

When you read about fraud globally from credible sources (like accounting firms or banks), the data they are pulling is almost always from a report called the ACFE (Report to the Nations). If it's not where they are getting data from, it should be. www.acfe.com.

 The ACFE reports are based on over 2500 real cases of employee fraud.

The first time I read the report, I was absolutely amazed at how thorough, professional, and easy-to-understand it was.

The reports are based on over 2500 real cases of fraud, in order to find the most effective methods for reducing fraud and fraud losses. They use data from 133 countries and there are 23 major industries in listed categories. It shows the highest median losses by industry, profiles of fraudsters, and provides enough useable metrics to allow for a substantial and useable red flag listing. This will assist everyone in finding the most effective methods for minimizing and reducing fraud and losses as a result.

In summary, the ACFE reports do not just call out facts and

percentages, but also look for constant ways and measures to mitigate and stop fraud. The information has a purpose and not just a metric.

In most presentations, reports are the boring overheads or statistics that we won't remember. I can tell you that some of the reports, metrics and statistics could save your business.

When the time came that I actually realized how many businesses are being affected by employee based fraud and how much there is, it pains me to say that once it has happened there's not much you can do about it. Fraud cases are complicated, difficult and expensive to investigate and are very time consuming. If I am sounding negative, that's because there's nothing to protect you once it has happened. That's why the book and the presentation is called "Just Look". If the rights systems are put into place along with employee awareness and then you add just a little common sense, the likelihood of fraud diminishes greatly.

The number of small to mid-sized companies hit with employee-based fraud is growing all the time, and this is where my experience lies, and so will be my focus.

I know that a few of the topics will sound very boring, such as discussing a balance sheet? I mean, really?!

Hopefully, once you see how the balance sheet can be used to avoid scrutiny, you will want to at least have it on your radar. I wish someone had made me just look.

One thing, before we get into anything.

There are a few key things you need to know:

1) You need to stop fraud before it happens at your business. Once it has happened, there is nothing much you can do and the likelihood of recovery is slim at best.

2) 10 % of people at work will not steal from you. 10% are probably stealing right now. The remaining 80% could go either way depending on the risk level of getting caught.

3) If someone hasn't taken a holiday in two or three years, they are stealing from you.

I hope this helps someone and entertains you a little.

INTRODUCTION
JUST LOOK!! INTERNAL CONTROL WEAKNESSES

JUST LOOK!!

I want these two words to resonate every time somebody who has been to one of my presentations or read through this book walks by something at the office that just doesn't look right, when they see something that looks a little off or different or when something looks odd or unusual. Instead of just leaving and shrugging it off, I hope they remember my two words. **Just Look!!**

I want it to make them stop and **Just Look!!**

Let's say they look at where the company checks are stored and see company checks are out of sequence or they see a staff member filling up two cars on the same day, or maybe when they see credit card statements that have been photocopied and sections cut out or when someone has not taken a vacation in over two years they will stop and look.

If something looks like a chicken and sounds like a chicken… it probably is a chicken.

Just Look!! I wish I had Just Looked…

INTERNAL CONTROL WEAKNESSES: POOR OVERSIGHT, POOR TONE AT THE TOP AND OTHER RANTS

Internal Control Weaknesses, Poor Oversight and Poor Tone at the Top. Just like the title and sub-title say.

They all mean the same thing. **Just Look!** Watch your back and put something in place to protect you.

I was looking through one of my recent versions of the book and I pieced together a few paragraphs and sentences that didn't quite fit where they were but also had great information in them. I also wanted to get some of my ranting out of the way early. So here we go.

In business I know at times I have felt over my head, and any kind of success seemed to come with great learning opportunities. I didn't go to school for business or business management, but I was good with people. I used to say all the time that I wanted to find someone to help us run the financial and administrative end of things. Or, possibly, that we should find someone to run the company for us while I focused on sales and customer relationships.

I know I'm not alone as I still hear this a lot from other business owners. It doesn't work, and it doesn't exist.

 Please let this resonate. If you could find anyone that could run your company for you at the level you would need them at, they would be a competitor, not an employee.

In my case, it seemed the more freedom I had, the more I looked the other way, or put my head in the sand.

For the first time in over 12 years, the company was losing money. We couldn't put our fingers on why, but I know now…

Someone was stealing. Not just because I wasn't looking, but because I was looking for answers for the loss everywhere except where I needed to.

Simply put, I had poor oversight (or no oversight).

We had every red flag popping up to suggest fraud. I just didn't look. In hindsight, I trusted much more than I should have.

I know now that if you are not going to look yourself, that's ok, but you need to have control systems in place that are looking for you.

Instead of examining our financials and areas of operations (such as cash flow, income statements, and balance sheets), I started to study what was wrong with my way of management or leadership. I spent my time looking for a way to improve how I ran the company. I spent time meditating, doing tai chi, reading about how the brain works… everything except what seems obvious now, looking at and reviewing the financial details of the business.

~

THE BUSINESS IS LOSING MONEY? OK, I WILL STUDY THE BRAIN….. INSTEAD OF ACTUALLY LOOKING AT THE FINANCIALS! YES, THAT'S A GREAT IDEA!

~

DON'T ASSUME ANYTHING:

I would like anyone reading along or listening to my presentations to realize how slow and frustrating the process is for the victim of fraud. To avoid a long and traumatic experience like ours, you have to put measures in place to prevent fraud and know where you need to look to find it. People say to me all the time, well you trusted this person. How would you know, I mean you have to be able to trust people. I always respond, just because you leave your door open at your house doesn't mean somebody should steal everything, however, that's why we have alarms, locks on our doors and exterior lighting. They are safe guards in place to protect us and our investments and assets. That's also why we put salt or sand on ice in the winter.

In our experience, we seemed to have an open and shut case. The amount of evidence, witnesses, and paper trail was excessive. Surely the fraudster would admit to the crime and we would recoup some of the stolen money and get back to doing business. I assumed the criminal courts would lock up the defendant's finances and make sure none of the money moved around while the trial took place.

I mean, it was so obvious.

Boy, was I wrong! Even though we had piles of irrefutable and substantiative evidence, the former employee was never going to admit to the crime, even when handed proof. The first line of the statement that was read by the the first batch of defence lawyers said something like this:

 "John told me he was the Devil and that he killed his father". I will just leave that with you....

That was a surprise when we first heard it. WOW! Then, we have to expect this type of thing. Nothing surprised us. It was almost like any new stunts and schemes anyone had to delay, frustrate or distract would be tested here. That was until far into the days of the final trial, the Crown had rested long ago and the questioning went to the Defendant. I do not remember the exact words used but let me say the Defendant eluded that I had made unwanted personal, even sexual advances. Keep in mind, this is 8 years or so into the case and in the final days of the final trial. This was the very first time anyone connected to the court had heard this and there was no evidence or anyone else who was told or had been told ever.

That's not to say, people who are victims have to come out immediately or they are not credible. It is serious and should be taken as such.

I am a lot of things, that is not in my scope of possibility, it obviously never happened and we were all very sickened by the depths someone would go. The court room got a little noisy at that point and the Crown Attorney jumped up, as did almost everyone else and called out what is known as the *Browne v. Dunn* principal.

Basically the rule states that a party cannot lead testimony in chief from its witness that contradicts or impeaches the evidence of the opponent's witness in a material particular without having cross-examined that witness on the same matter. In layman's terms, if you say or bring forward something that will deliberately cause prejudice to your opponent, you should have brought that to the witness while he or she was on the stand and had a chance to defend or at least deny it.

The Judge was very upset and said the statement would be removed or 'weighted" very low due to the nature in which it was brought forward. On its own, and random.

The next person on the stand was a 21 year old pregnant girl who I worked with for years and she stood firm and said she had never seen or heard anything like that about me. She adamantly stated my character was not one that walked in those pathways. That was an insane afternoon. Again, not to say someone cannot bring things forward after years. They can and do, it is that this was brought as a Hail Mary throw in desperation to bring my character into question, without a stick of any evidence to consistency in the testimony. Just when I thought I had seen it all. I mean, that's a new low.

They had subpoena'd repeatedly anyone they didn't want in the court room and never called them as witness but it also prevented them from entering the courtroom during other testimonies. They subpoena'd a truckload of records from CRA and called two or three auditors as witnesses. I feel in order to try and scare us all and make us nervous like they had something.

They put this person in handcuffs and walked them out of the courtroom to serve a penitentiary sentence, and yet the perpetrator of this crime has still denied any wrongdoing. As I write this, it is almost 2023 and we still have yet to gain full access to the funds and assets that we had frozen over a decade ago.

The bottom line is I had poor oversight and a non-existent control system in place.

Looking at the statistics on the accompanying chart, internal control weaknesses contribute to occupational fraud. I can see that we lacked all of the internal controls needed to responsibly navigate a business of our size **(see FiG AC-1).**

What is an Internal Control Weakness?

Internal control weaknesses are various factors that can facilitate a perpetrator's ability to commit and conceal an occupational or employee-based fraud.

These include a lack of reporting mechanisms, having no clear lines of authority, not implementing an ongoing employee fraud education program, having no independent checks or audits as well as not placing competent personnel in oversight positions. This is also referred to as a poor tone at the top.

If that's poor tone, then boy I was tone-deaf! This was the primary risk factor in 22% of all financial statement frauds based on the ACFE report. I wasn't good at reviewing and digging deeper into financials.

The trial and pre-trial went on for years and years. One of the reasons I'm speaking publicly about this, and one of the reasons I wrote this book was to try to save others from some of the headaches and frustrations we encountered over the 10 to 12 years of the trial. The legal system is built to be fair, but it allows for what I call "gaming" or manipulation of the system. Every new judgement of a trial becomes a precedent for those that follow, so it can be a big turning wheel that just keeps reiterating the same things over and over.

 Fraud defence lawyers now have a tool-belt or an arsenal of many different tactics that can be used to delay, exhaust and sometimes even have things thrown out. Some fraud defence lawyers are even listing possible methods of defence right on their website so fraudsters or would-be fraudsters would be able to use this as a source as well.

In this book, I will review some of the different techniques that fraudsters use to commit crimes and how we can put measures in place to identify them and prevent them from happening. I will also go over different parts of the law that pertain to employee based fraud, both in the criminal sense and relating to the charter of rights, which is becoming more important to understand than ever.

I will review red flags (or warning signs) as well as suggest some actions that can be put in place to help mitigate fraud. I will also review a few different actual cases that make reference to areas of the law or the charter of rights where it pertains to fraud. I find that this helps clarify in real world situations, some of the different areas of fraud and fraud related laws.

I will examine the relationship I feel that owners need to have with their balance sheet and overall financial statements. I believe it is vital for business owners to at the very least, understand how it works. That's where the fraud was hidden in our case. As you will see later in the book, the accounting area of fraud can be one of the many reasons that frauds don't make it through the courts. The examination of financial records can be extremely time consuming and labor intensive for the courts, in relation to preparing for trial. Time consuming and labor intensive also means expensive. I will also touch on what mechanisms may be available to recover your funds after a guilty verdict when restitution is part of the sentencing.

"So, just print out your entire accounting records for the last 20 years. It should be about 5 million sheets of paper and let us know when it's ready...

One of the tactics some defence law firms make in employee fraud cases is asking for accounting paperwork. In our case, they asked for entire payroll records, in fact, the entire accounting records in paper form. If you understand anything about accounting at all, you'll know about linked accounts and how one transaction can connect to many others, and none of it would make sense printed out. That's why they asked for it; it would tie up valuable time and resources. When they asked for the accounting records, the judge looked to us to see if we could supply that.

Judges and crown attorneys are not accountants and may not and should not understand all of the intricacies of accounting records. This presents a golden opportunity for an accused fraudster to delay, outlast and frustrate the system in an attempt to have their case thrown out. Some defendants ask for things they know don't exist, like entire email records or accounting backups ... again just to create lengthy delays.

In our case, the defendant claimed repeatedly that they couldn't open up the Records of Accounting software on their computer. Another delay tactic.

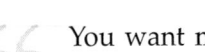

 ❝ You want me to testify and explain the execution of the fraud?

After 7-8 years had passed, the people at the accounting firm that had worked on the records and uncovered the actual methods of fraud in the full forensic report did not recall everything. I ended up personally taking the stand to present the details of the technical end of the fraud and, in turn, took questions and redress from the defence. It made me better understand technically how it was done and I knew that I had to explain it in layman's terms so everyone could understand it ...

The Head Crown Attorney in charge actually brought us in at one point and told us that he was going to just pursue charges of credit card fraud, and that we could go after the rest through civil means. This means we would have to pay a civil law firm to chase after the fraudsters. This was in frustration since the accused was tying up valuable court resources. Thankfully one of the members of our team protested very loudly, and we ended up staying the course.

As mentioned, I assumed early on that the accused would not be able to move money or that their assets would be frozen. However, in order to do this, you have to have a civil trial (and pay an expensive civil team), and get judges to sign orders. In the amount of time it takes just to get a court date, defendants can move and disperse money at will.

As you'll see later, there is a law where if the fraudster can try to prove that they are impecunious (or without funds), they can actually request access to funds that may have been frozen in civil court, to use for their legal expenses. If this is successful, the money you have spent on legal fees is lost, as well as the money you've had frozen. If the defence wins here, this is a vicious circle and the victim is victimized again and again with no recourse and no voice.

We were lucky that our fraud happened in a smaller municipality. I read recently that companies experiencing fraud in larger city centres were less likely to get to trial, let alone get a conviction. Many don't even get in front of a judge.

In our case the defence retained 4-5 different law firms, only to fire each one. We saw trial dates in 3 different levels of court, Provincial, Federal, and Appeals. We saw every delay imaginable.

Defendants can also fire their attorneys at will, even on the first day of a trial in order to get a delay. They can also ask to be moved to a different level of court at any moment because it's their right!

I want to be clear. I'm not writing this as an authority, but as someone who has been there on the front lines. Some of you may already have measures in place to protect your business from fraud, and you should feel good about that.

Many old-school business owners who are hands-on seem to navigate a business career with little or no fraud. However, trouble can happen at times when a company is growing. It is necessary to put people in place to look after things like finance, banking, receivables, customer service, and even sales. There are a few very simple things that any of us can do to mitigate fraud or even prevent it. This is not to say it won't happen. If the person committing the fraud has control of the paperwork, financials, and narrative, they can play shell games with items on the balance sheet and even hide cheques that have been written. If they control the narrative, they can even keep this from your valued accountants.

If you had told me 15 years ago that someone I trusted was going to steal over three quarters of a million dollars from my company I would have said you're crazy. Someone would have seen it. We have a book-keeper and accounting firm doing review engagements for the bank, which is examined quarterly. If someone told me that the same person was going to have their children on payroll and have maxed out company credit cards, I would've said the same thing again.

I know better now. An accountant's job is not to dig and recall digital copies of cheques in the pursuit of fraudulent activity. Nor is it their responsibility to ensure that all purchase orders, bills, and payroll records are legitimate. If something is out of balance, accountants will ask for a backup of that specific account. However, if the fraudster controls the systems, they can deliver a version of the data that has been manipulated to avoid scrutiny.

You'll see later on that dreams like restitution orders, fine in lieu and asset forfeitures all sound good, but are as rare as a unicorn. What really happens in Canada after a fraud is uncovered is that you have to pay civil lawyers to look for and freeze assets or get non-dissipate orders in order to have the possibility of any recovery.

As I mentioned, there are many playbooks or games used in the defence against fraud.

One tactic is to simply not show up to civil appearances. The plaintiff pays for preparation and legal representation for that date, and all those expenses are lost, and the defendant loses nothing. In our case this happened too many times to mention. Again, I assumed that the judges would impose penalties for this, but nothing happened. The focus instead is on the defendants getting a fair trial. This seems to supersede any measures to assist the corporations or small businesses that have been defrauded.

∿

Here's your free standing restitution order. Good luck
with all that...

Most Restitution orders handed out in Canada are what's called
Freestanding or Stand Alone. I will say, it's better to have one than not
but it would help the victims if there were some form of timeline and
punishment if it is not repaid. Especially when the victim has had
money stolen. The standalone restitutions turn responsibility over to
the victims to pay for civil lawyers, investigators, and reports in order
to try to recoup money.

It is my opinion that judges rarely hand out anything other than a
free-standing restitution order because at the end of their tenure, if
they handed out say 100 restitution orders, they would need to address
them and possibly review them with new judges coming in to fill their
shoes. In essence, they are leaving the cases open and that adds a lot of
work for them. It's easier to hand out the free standing order than one
with terms and conditions. Just my opinion.

A stand-alone restitution order **has no time limit for repayment
and may be registered as a civil judgement which in turn could be
used to garnish wages and seize property**. The purpose of Restitution
is that it is intended to rehabilitate the offender by making them immediately responsible for the loss of the victim.

We spoke with the Crown attorneys office many times about something called **fine-in-lieu**. This is a great idea. We were told this is a
legal option that would make fraudsters think twice about dragging a
trial on and on. For example, if victims are granted a restitution order
for $500,000 and it isn't paid back within four years, the defendant
could face a year in prison for each $100,000 not repaid. This might be
a great deterrent, however in our case, it was more of a legend than the
aforementioned unicorn. At the end of the book, you will find a case
where the judge actually made fine-in-lieu enforceable.

There seems to be two camps of thinking that are forming. One is to
pursue civil action first and then report to the police and crown if
needed. The quick strike does have positives, such as window to locate

funds before they are moved and the likelihood of settlement has a better chance this way. However, the costs can add up. The victim is rarely considered in the criminal trials. I've heard more victims lately after being dragged through the criminal system say "I just want my money, I don't care what happens to them criminally!"

 Maybe there is a light at the end of this very long tunnel.

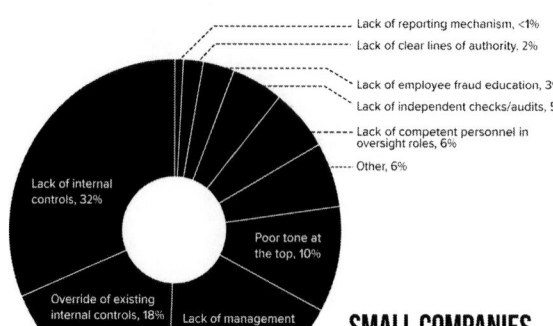

Internal Control Weaknesses That Contribute to Occupational Fraud

Various factors can facilitate a perpetrator's ability to commit and conceal an occupational fraud scheme.

WHAT ARE THE PRIMARY INTERNAL CONTROL WEAKNESSES THAT CONTRIBUTE TO OCCUPATIONAL FRAUD?

- Lack of reporting mechanism, <1%
- Lack of clear lines of authority, 2%
- Lack of employee fraud education, 3%
- Lack of independent checks/audits, 5%
- Lack of competent personnel in oversight roles, 6%
- Other, 6%

Lack of internal controls, 32%

Poor tone at the top, 10%

Override of existing internal controls, 18%

Lack of management review, 18%

MANAGER-LEVEL PERPETRATORS
are more likely than other perpetrators to **OVERRIDE EXISTING CONTROLS**

Employees	15%
Managers	**22%**
Owner/executives	17%

SMALL COMPANIES
are more likely to **lack internal controls**

LARGE COMPANIES
are more likely to have **controls overridden**

Lack of internal controls
- 43%
- 28%

Override of existing internal controls
- 12%
- 20%

■ <100 employees
□ 100+ employees

POOR TONE AT THE TOP
was the primary risk factor in 22% of all financial statement frauds.

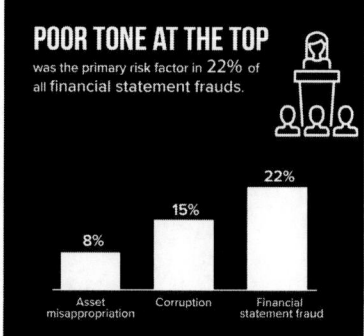

- Asset misappropriation: 8%
- Corruption: 15%
- Financial statement fraud: 22%

SOLE PERPETRATORS take advantage of a lack of controls, while schemes involving **COLLUSION** are supported by poor tone at the top and an ability to override controls

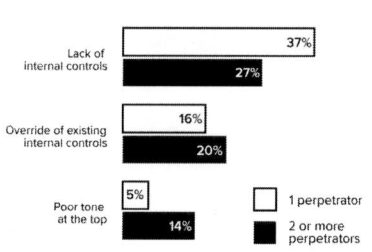

Lack of internal controls
- 37%
- 27%

Override of existing internal controls
- 16%
- 20%

Poor tone at the top
- 5%
- 14%

□ 1 perpetrator
■ 2 or more perpetrators

36 **Victim Organizations** Report to the Nations

FIG AC-1 Source: 2020 Report to the Nations. Copyright 2020 by the Association of Certified Fraud Examiners, Inc

CHAPTER I
UNCOVERING A FRAUD

> *One day you wake up and just like any other day, you grab a coffee and go to work. Then, there's a knock at the door and one of your colleagues asks if you can spare a few minutes. There's something you need to take a look at.........*

~

I truly hope none of you ever have to experience this scenario.

I was at our temporary office in the board room with a customer and I remember looking out the window noticing that our bookkeeper was coming in. About 5 minutes later, I saw them leave.

There was a knock on the boardroom door. It was our Vice President, looking like he had seen a ghost. He asked if I could come and look at something. That's where it all began.....

I have asked the former VP if he would like to add something here. In his own words, here's how he uncovered the fraud.

. . .

"**A**fter suffering a devastating fire that destroyed our Company's main office and production facility, we spent the remaining months of that year attempting to maintain and rebuild the company while entrusting the majority of our day-to-day operations to a trusted employee. During this time, we pivoted, due to the fire, to a completely outsourced supply chain. Prior to the fire we had controlled the majority of production internally while managing outsourced suppliers as well. Another colleague worked daily with the Insurance Company while I focused on our customers and keeping the business functioning. Our employees assisted in vendor relations while controlling incoming insurance payments and revenues and keeping our outsourced partners paid, in addition to our internal staff costs.

As the dust began to settle and the months moved along, (as did the Insurance process,) I approached our employees on several occasions regarding access to our accounting system. Over the past several years, my account visibility was limited after we had changed Accounting Systems, which was fine, as during that time there was little need for high visibility. That's why we had brought in an employee. However, in starting fresh and rebuilding the company, it felt like the right time to become more involved in the financial workings of the company, as I had been in the past.

It was discussed that my task would be to determine what our operating costs and expenses were prior to, and after the fire. For this I would need access to all areas.

Several attempts over a number of weeks, requesting full access to our Accounting Software were always either diverted to other issues to be dealt with, or left with the message that our employee had reached out to our Book Keeper to change the access, as they were the one who controlled that and not the employee. I rarely saw or spoke with our Book Keeper and my day-to-day was busy enough managing the rebuild after the fire and maintaining business and customer relations, so contacting our Book Keeper was often an after-thought. I would simply pass on another message to our former employee to pass on.

After an extended length of time, I became frustrated and just happened to run into our Book Keeper in our office one day. When I immediately inquired as to why my access to our Accounting system was still limited, and why they hadn't responded to our colleagues request to open my access, the reply was that they had never received such a request. Then they politely opened our Accounting Software and within seconds said, "there you go, you have full access now".

Within the hour, I had opened our system and the first thing that came up was Company Payroll.

~

Scrolling through the screen, within minutes I noticed the employee's family members name on the company payroll. Reviewing the file, I was shocked to see that in this previous year, the family member had earned a larger income than me! Even stranger than that...they were not even employed with us.

~

This was on a Friday afternoon and by Sunday evening we had uncovered mountains of fraudulent transactions ranging from Payroll to Vendor Invoices/Payments, Home Renovation expenses, furniture, Visa/Amex transactions for family vacations, jewelry... the list goes on to the sum of almost $750k.

Most of these transactions were very well hidden, disguised, and authorized solely by our employee, who controlled the Income/Expenses exclusively while having signing authority."

After being shown the accounting records, I was shocked and I suggested that before we jump to conclusions, we need to take it to the person in question and simply ask them. We need to handle it as calmly as possible. If there was a plausible explanation and we had approached it in an accusatory tone, and we were wrong, we would've felt terrible and looked even worse.

So, taking my advice, my colleague went and calmly asked the employee about what they found. Sure enough, an hour later, I got a phone call. My colleague indicated that everything was fine and thank goodness we didn't jump to conclusions. The year wasn't done yet and there were all sorts of things that still needed to be entered.

I was pleased, however, something was not sitting right with me. I wanted to check one thing before I took the explanation as fact. I asked our VP to review everyone's payroll records to see if they were all in the same state of disarray.

The next call came 20 minutes later. All the other records looked just as they should be, nothing out of the ordinary.

I immediately had the accounting records locked, changed passwords and drove the data to our accountant, where they began a forensic audit looking for fraud.

The team at the accounting firm initially followed the trail in the balance sheet and payroll records. They reviewed cancelled cheques, credit card statements, and any other relevant records.

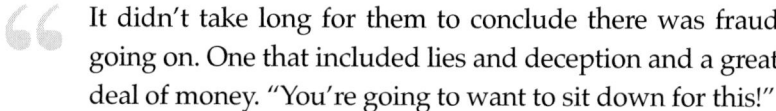

It didn't take long for them to conclude there was fraud going on. One that included lies and deception and a great deal of money. "You're going to want to sit down for this!"

When news about the fraud was first announced in the local newspaper, responses fell mainly within three categories.

1) Empathy/Kindness

"I can't believe this happened to you! You must be devastated. I hope you're able to recover some funds."

2) Frustration

"John, what were you thinking? Come on, you weren't watching your money! You know better than that."

As much as it may pain me to say it, they were right!

The 2020 Report to the Nations from the ACFE (Association of Certified Fraud Examiners) called this "internal control weakness" (see

Fig AC-1). This contributes to occupational or employee fraud due to the following: a lack of reporting mechanisms, no clear lines of authority, limited employee fraud education, the absence of independent checks and balances and a lack of any over-sight/management review.

I mean, call it like it is, I wasn't paying attention to the finances, my focus was on sales. What if I had implemented any of these controls? Not to say it wouldn't have happened, but If it did, it would have <u>been</u> on a much smaller scale.

3) The third response was "Are you going to sue your Accountant?" The simple answer is "NO!" It was not my accountant's fault.

Some people were of the opinion that if we paid a larger accounting firm to do bookkeeping, they should have caught this fraud.

I will go into a little more detail later in the book about this. It's important for business owners to know what the accountants do and what they are responsible for.

We had an internal book keeper, staff who worked on files, and an accountant who did our year end, and with whom we had quarterly meetings to review. Surely, somebody would have seen something.

Many people think accounting firms watch every move, and during year-end or monthly reviews anything out of the ordinary should come to light. That's just not true. A complex fraud can be hidden so successfully that it takes forensic accounting firms sometimes months, if not years to uncover.

I went into the trial and the whole experience with certain assumptions, ones that I know other people involved also had. We thought that assets would be frozen, and the accused would be under scrutiny, making sure money was not moving around. But none of that happened.

There is a way of putting liens on properties, putting what is called writs of seizure sale or writs of execution and freezing of assets, but it is expensive. In Canada, in order to do this, the victim must hire a civil law firm to go after the fraudster. Court dates must be arranged and the Judges have to approve all orders.

If I knew then what I know now, my expectations would have been much more grounded. I assumed that it would go quickly because we had a lot of clear-cut evidence. I assumed the criminal justice system would lock up everything this person had and either freeze or limit their accounts.

I found out rather quickly that my assumptions were not correct.

The accused can use the fact that the victim has to pay for a civil attorney to their benefit. In order to get searches, liens, and subpoenas done, the victim has to pay civil lawyers, and and if the defence loses civil costs for the trial cannot be recouped by a criminal court order.

The defence team can use this to their advantage simply by having their client not show up for civil trials or discoveries.

The defendants in our civil case did not show up for more than 60% of their dates. We had to pay our law firm for preparation and representation at each date while the accused would simply not show and faced no consequences. The trial judge would never hand down a penalty for it, even though he was frustrated.

 At times it seemed that the courts walked on eggshells, trying not to crack the human and civil rights shell of the fraudster.

It is an exhausting experience and not that uncommon. Later in the book I will discuss a recent trial where a lawyer suggests not even considering the criminal process until all civil measures have been exhausted.

Early in our trial, the Crown Attorney discussed actions that may increase the likelihood of financial recovery as well as act as a possible deterrent. This is known as fine-in-lieu; extra jail time for unpaid restitution. There was also talk of asset forfeiture and other remedies, but I soon realized these were practically fiction and not really enforceable, nor did it seem that the judges were confident in handing them out. The judges have things they can do to help he victims, like putting enforcement mechanisms in place and penalties if repayment isn't done in a set amount of time. I think the Judges would rather have the case dealt with. Otherwise, they would have hundreds of open files.

Toward the end of our case, a charter act (specifically 11b) was instituted to shorten timelines and make cases run through the system much quicker. There were cases in Canada being stayed (basically thrown out for taking too long).

Charter 11b

Any person charged with an offence has the right to be tried within a reasonable time.

18 months for provincial courts and 30 months for Superior.

Later on in the book, I'll highlight real-world examples of Fine-in-lieu, Restitution and Asset Forfeiture in different cases and decisions. I will discuss the Charter of Rights acts and decisions that will affect businesses and their owners going forward.

Many times, crimes like fraud go unpunished and don't even make it to trial because the owners of the companies do not want to bring that kind of press onto their organization. Embarrassment is a contributing factor.

What I hope to do with this book is to save business owners the time and aggravation we had to endure. I won't lie, it was traumatic. It is traumatic and fraud can ruin lives.

There are very simple things that can help. Small procedures and preventative actions put in place will slowly tighten all the bolts.

Our case dragged on for over 10 years. There were too many civil and criminal appearances to even list. The cost was heavy on the taxpayer and the families involved. The defence switched lawyers during the trial many times because it was their right to do so. We spent over $28,000 in civil legal fees to block the defence from obtaining money to pay their legal fees, the same funds we had to pay to have frozen in civil court. During the trial, while they plead poverty and asked for legal aid (after racking up exorbitant legal fees hiring and firing numerous high profile lawyers), they proceeded to buy a property outright without any legal consequences. We were able to get a freeze order on the property and it's been 11 years since that order and we are still trying to get our hands on that property. They had not paid property tax on it and let it go into arrears, so we had to pay the taxes to prevent the property from being sold in a Sheriffs sale.

I believe the Canadian justice system has slowly been writing a hand book on how to get away with fraud. Some of the recent decisions and Charter of Rights discussions seem to almost take the side of the criminal. I understand they do this to make sure innocent people do not go to jail, but in doing so, the victim and the victims families are often ignored. These things to help the defendants are put in place to help the one person who has a case and honestly wants to clear their name asap. I am not suggesting it's purposeful. I truly believe from first hand experience, the people working in the Canadian justice system want to do the right thing.

These laws and Charter Acts are put in place to protect people who truly want to defend themselves, not to cause delays and play games in an attempt to exasperate the system.

In the coming chapters we will answer the question, what is fraud? We will review the profile of a fraudster, discuss red flags and warning signs of fraud, and look at how to minimize risks. I will review why it's important that every owner must understand the balance sheet and its relationship to the company. We will clarify the accountant's role in preparing statements, and what their liability is. We will dedicate an entire chapter to actions that can be taken to minimize, if not stop fraud from happening.

We will look over Canadian legal decisions as it pertains to fraud, the precedences that have been set from previous decisions, and the impact that has on the victims of fraud. I have attached FIG-AC-2 FROM the ACFE 2022 report below.

KEY FINDINGS

  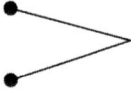

OUR STUDY COVERED

2,504 CASES
from
125 COUNTRIES

Causing total losses of more than
$3.6 BILLION

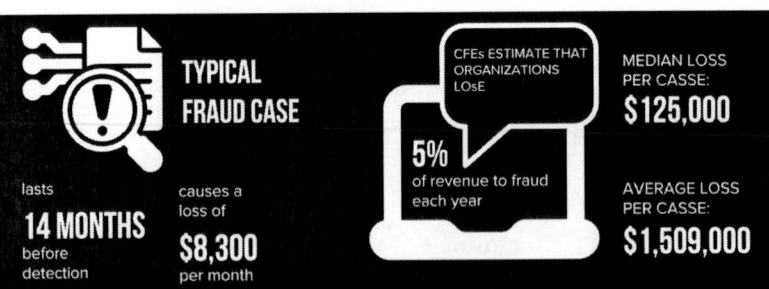

TYPICAL FRAUD CASE

lasts
14 MONTHS
before detection

causes a loss of
$8,300
per month

CFEs ESTIMATE THAT ORGANIZATIONS LOsE
5%
of revenue to fraud each year

MEDIAN LOSS PER CASSE:
$125,000

AVERAGE LOSS PER CASSE:
$1,509,000

CORRUPTION
WAS THE MOST COMMON SCHEME IN EVERY GLOBAL REGION

ASSETS MISAPPROPRIATION
schemes are the most common and least costly

86% of cases
$100,000 median loss

FINANCIAL STATEMENT FRAUD SCHEMES are the the least common and most costly

10% of cases
$954,000 median loss

Organizations with

FRAUD AWARENESS TRAINING
for employees were more likely to gather tips through

FORMAL REPORT MECHANISMS

56% of tips with training

37% of tips without training

43%

OF SCHEMES WERE DETECTED BY TIP.
and half of those tips came from employees

TELEPHONE HOTLINE and **E-MAIL**
were each used by whistleblowers in
33% of cases

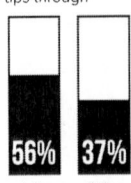 

FIG AC-2 Source: 2020 Report to the Nations. Copyright 2020 by the Association of Certified Fraud Examiners, Inc.

DENTISTS, CHIROPRACTORS, DOCTORS, AND VETS!

As I speak to more victims of employee- based fraud, I seem to be running into a certain type that is very common. This type of fraud lends itself to busy professional practices such as Dentists and Chiropractors. Places where there are a lot of appointments and where the Doctor or practitioner is too busy to deal with payments and transfers on their own.

One case in particular, occurred at a dental office where the employee who did the administration (including taking payments, checks, and transfers) had to leave for a week to go to a family function. The person filling in found a file that was full of E-TRANSFER/INTERAC payments from clients that appeared to need depositing. When she tried to route them to the dentist's bank account, it was discovered that all of them had been deposited already. E-transfers had been deposited into a personal bank account for quite some time; in fact, approximately one out of 10 was rerouted, equalling over $300,000 in theft. The individual who was stealing hadn't taken a holiday in five or six years. This is a major red flag.

Even General Surgeons could be vulnerable. When a procedure is elective (not covered by OHIP) people are required to pay personally. I had a small surgery lately and while I was at a follow-up appointment, I overheard the secretary tell a patient the the Doctor's policy for payment could only be cheques or cash. While there is nothing wrong with that, I think it could open the door for would be fraudsters.

JUST LOOK!

CHAPTER 2
WHAT IS FRAUD?

Cup Game

If *you operate a business, it's likely that at one time or another, you will be faced with employee fraud.*

Before we go any further, let's try to get a handle on what fraud means.

Fraud

Fraud is the wrongful or criminal deception intended to result in financial or personal gain. The definition of Fraud is left ambiguous in order to capture the vast nature that these offences occur. There are many examples of Fraud, but most commonly seen are Telemarketing scams, online scams, Identity Theft and Business scams.

Section Wording

Everyone who, by deceit, falsehood or other fraudulent means, whether or not it is a false pretense within the meaning of this Act, defrauds the public or any person, whether ascertained or not, of any property, money or valuable security or any service, (a) is guilty of an indictable offence and liable to a term of imprisonment not exceeding fourteen years, where the subject-matter of the offence is a testamentary instrument or the value of the subject-matter of the offence exceeds five thousand dollars; or (b) is guilty (i) of an indictable offence and is liable to imprisonment for a term not exceeding two years, or (ii) of an offence punishable on summary conviction, where the value of the subject-matter of the offence does not exceed five thousand dollars.

ACFE Report

The 2020 ACFE report covered **2504** cases from **125** countries. Just those **2504** cases caused a loss of more than **$3.6 billion**. The typical fraud went on for **14** months before detection and caused an average loss of **$8,300** a month. It is estimated that 5% of company revenues are lost due to fraud and the median loss per case is **$125,000**.

Certain frauds are more likely in small to mid-size businesses. Billing Fraud is two times higher, while payroll fraud and cheque and payment tampering are four times higher. Men committed 72% of all employer occupational fraud at an average loss of $150,000, while female perpetrated fraud saw an average $85,000 loss.

Executives committed only 20% of frauds but caused the largest losses at an average of $600,000, while managers averaged $150,000. More than half of all occupational fraud comes from these four departments: operations, accounting, management, and sales.

According to the 2020 ACFE:

- 80% of fraudsters faced some form of internal discipline from the victim's organization;

- 46% of victim organizations declined to refer cases to law enforcement because the internal discipline was sufficient;

- 42% of the fraudsters were living beyond their means;

- 26% of the fraudsters were experiencing financial difficulties.

I was initially going to title this chapter "What is Employee Based-Fraud?" However, I decided that before I do that, I should start with the definition of fraud and then go over how the Canadian criminal code describes it and defines it.

Here is a list of some common frauds in Canada:

Embezzlement

Tax fraud

Banking fraud

Internet fraud

Medical fraud

Insurance fraud

Credit card fraud

Identity theft

Canada's Criminal Code provides a general description of potential fraud to allow for a wide degree of discretion in Fraud.

Most cases of criminal fraud are addressed by Section 380(1) of the Criminal Code. Credit card fraud charges are sometimes under Section 342, which covers credit card theft and credit card fraud. Usually, Tax fraud is under Section 239 of Canada's Income Tax Act.

Fraud According to the Criminal Code

Section 380(1) of the Criminal Code has a two-part definition to describe fraud: 1) a prohibited act of "deceit, falsehood or other fraudulent means;" and 2) that this act deprives the public or specific person of "any property, money or valuable security, or any service."

Intent

The Code cites "intent" as a critical component of fraud charges. Legal precedents set by previous Canadian court cases mandate that the Crown must prove intent in order to secure a conviction. This means that someone can be charged for the intent to commit fraud, even if they were unsuccessful.

Standard of Proof & Reasonable Doubt

The standard of proof in a Canadian criminal trial means "proof beyond a reasonable doubt".

In a criminal case, the prosecution (Crown) bears the burden of proving that the defendant is guilty beyond all reasonable doubt. This means that the prosecution must convince the judge or jury that there is no other reasonable explanation that can come from the evidence presented at trial. In other words, the judge or jury must be certain of the defendant's guilt in order to render a guilty verdict. This standard of proof is much higher than the civil standard, called "preponderance of the evidence," which only requires a certainty greater than 50 percent.

In Canada, it's not up to the defendant or their lawyers to prove their innocence. At the very minimum, it's good enough for them just to argue that the crown has failed to prove the case beyond a reasonable doubt. In the Canadian system, everybody's presumed innocent until proven guilty. The idea of reasonable doubt is wrapped up with the presumption of innocence.

Penalties for Criminal Fraud

In Canada, there are basically two forms of fraud in regard to charges. Fraud over $5000 or Fraud under $5000

Penalties are based on the value of the fraud. Values greater than $5,000 can result in a maximum prison sentence of up to 14 years. If the value exceeds $1 million, the minimum sentence is two years imprisonment. Fraud involving property valued at less than $5,000 will receive an entry on the fraudsters criminal record, may receive a fine and a prison sentence of up to a maximum of two years.

In determining penalties, courts consider a number of factors listed by the Criminal Code. These include:

- **Number of victims**

- Impact on the victim(s)

- Complexity and degree of planning the offender took to commit the fraud

- Degree in which the offender took advantage of their position within the community

- Destruction of records related to fraudulent activity

- Any impact on the Canadian economy or financial system

- Value of property involved (thus the two-year minimum sentence for values over $1 million).

When considering an appropriate sentence, Judges also consider mitigating factors, such as attempts at restitution, remorse, and whether the accused has an existing criminal record.

Most Common Types of Fraud

There are so many ways to deceive people, and since emerging technologies are always creating new ways to deceive, describing all types of fraud could fill a book. Some of the most common types of fraud include:

Embezzlement

Embezzlement is a type of fraud addressed under Section 322 of the Criminal Code covering theft. Most cases of embezzlement involve someone entrusted with property (usually money)—usually an employee—stealing through means of deceit. Embezzlement can be one-time or ongoing. Penalties for embezzlement call for a maximum prison sentence of up to 10 years for values greater than $5,000, and a maximum sentence of two years for embezzlement involving values less than $5,000. There is no mandatory minimum sentence for embezzlement and cases that are less than $5,000 can be addressed under the more lenient summary conviction category.

Tax Fraud

Tax fraud is usually under Section 239 of Canada's Income Tax Act and includes the deception, in writing or by a statement, to evade paying taxes or falsely claiming credits and/or refunds. Penalties can include fines and jail time of up to five years.

Mortgage Fraud

Mortgage fraud involves the misrepresentation of information to gain financing that otherwise would not be granted. There are many mortgage-based schemes, but all typically include assets and/or income being overstated. For example, providing misleading information about income sources and work details, or using false names on applications.

Medical Fraud

Medical fraud is when someone makes false claims and/or produces fake receipts to gain medical benefits from insurance companies. Medical fraud charges are under Section 380 of the Criminal Code.

Insurance Fraud

Knowingly lying on an insurance application or claim can lead to fraud charges, as can any attempt to deceptively claim damages. Charges relating to insurance fraud are under Section 380 of the Code.

Credit Card Fraud

Most credit card cases are addressed under Section 342 of the Criminal Code. Charges can be laid for possession, use, or selling of a credit card(s) that has been forged or altered. The maximum penalty for this is 10 years in prison.

Internet Fraud

Internet fraud is so common that fraud-related charges are liable to be laid under several different sections of the Criminal Code. Usually, 342 and 402.

WHAT IS EMPLOYEE BASED FRAUD?

Employee Based Fraud occurs when an employee commits fraud against their employer. The employer may be any form of business, including a sole proprietorship, partnership, corporation and organization.

While there are many kinds of employee fraud, the size and complexity of the fraud, and legal remedies are based on many factors, including:

- Amount of loss or damages
- Whether it was an isolated incident, or an ongoing complex scheme
- If the employee was put in a position of trust
- If the employee has a Fiduciary Duty or obligation to the employer

What Is a Fiduciary Duty?

A Fiduciary duty refers to the relationship between a fiduciary and the principal or beneficiary on whose behalf the fiduciary acts.

The fiduciary accepts legal responsibility for duties of care, loyalty, good faith, confidentiality, and more when serving the best interests of a beneficiary. Strict care must be taken to ensure that no conflict of interest arises to jeopardize those interests. An executive at a company or an accountant would have a Fiduciary Duty.

Common types of Employee based fraud

1. **Theft of Cash** - Stealing cash from an employer can take many forms, depending on the type of business.

2. **Unauthorized Billing and Overpayments** occur when an employee:
- transfers money into their own personal accounts
- falsely enters higher invoice amounts and keeps the over-payment
- issues false payments to their own accounts

3. **Kickbacks, Bribery, and Over-billing**

Fraud also occurs when an employee takes payments or benefits from, or over-billing, in exchange for providing business advantages to a company, such as clients or suppliers.

4. Benefits Fraud

Benefits fraud can be committed by an individual or by a large group of employees

5. Workers' Compensation Fraud

This involves an employee exaggerating injuries, inventing injuries that did not occur, or claiming injuries that occurred at home actually happened at work, in order to receive compensation.

6. Asset Misappropriation

This is the theft of company assets by an employee and can include many types of fraud, such as:

- using a company credit card for personal use, using company equipment for personal use, forging or altering a company cheque, theft of cash or inventory and submitting inflated expense claims

- using a company expense account for personal reasons and submitting them as company expenses, and personal use of company vehicles

7. Payroll Fraud

Payroll fraud involves a theft using the company's payroll system, and can include keeping a non-existent employee on the payroll and diverting that pay to their account, altering time sheets to inflate hours, clocking in and out for someone else or inflating hours on a timesheet, or stealing someone else's pay cheque and cashing it.

8. Intellectual Property Theft

This is when an employee steals data or trade secrets (called intellectual property). This can include stealing information to sell to a competitor or downloading a company's contacts to use or sell.

According to the Association of Certified Fraud Examiners (ACFE), a typical company will lose approximately five percent of its annual revenue to fraudulent activities. However, the losses associated with fraud typically extend far beyond the misappropriated cash and other company assets, such as reputational damage, lost productivity, loss of future opportunities, and the cost of accounting audits. In addition, fraud can take a huge a toll on morale.

The shock of knowing that a trusted employee or colleague was capable of such deceit can build up further mistrust and interfere with staff's ability to focus on their job functions. Additionally, being associated with a company undergoing a fraud investigation is often embarrassing for employees.

Employee fraud is defined by the ACFE as 'the use of one's occupation for personal enrichment through the deliberate misuse or misapplication of the employing organization's resources or assets,' and is often the by-product of opportunity.

More types of Employee based or Occupational fraud:

Accounts Receivable Fraud

Accounts receivable fraud can ruin a company financially. Of course, the fraud itself is harmful to finances, but the stigma attached to fraud can have a negative impact on customer relations.

The accounts receivable process can be a playground for fraud if the right checks and balances aren't in place. Fraudsters will often create and leave paper trails to mislead investigators. An employee will use any concealing tactic they can to balance the books and hide the fraud: stealing paper statements, adding discounts, and applying payments to the wrong accounts.

Lapping Fraud

Lapping is a form of A/R (Accounts receivable) Fraud.

Lapping can easily be elaborate and is best explained by example.

Samuel works for a company that provides evestrough and window cleaning services. He is the sole member of the A/R team and, recently, has been going through a hard time financially. One day, Samuel gets a $1000 cheque from Customer X. Samuel pockets the check. A few days later, another customer sends in a $1000 cheque as well. Samuel uses the check from Customer Y and credits it to Customer X's account to replace the missing $1000 payment.

Samuel now has an extra $1000 in his pocket and Customer X's account has balanced out with the payment from Customer Y. Customer Y's account is still in the negatives until the next Customer's money comes in. This is a walking time bomb. Samuel will continue doing this, robbing Peter to pay Paul with the account until the scheme is found out (likely) or he pays back the money (unlikely).

Uncovering Lapping Fraud

The person committing this type of fraud usually ends up caving under the pressure. The sheer volume of transactions will overwhelm them. They eventually slip and expose it on their own.

Lapping is a popular way to conceal a skimming fraud.

Skimming Fraud

Skimming fraud is done before the payment enters the company's accounting system and is what separates it from cash larceny. Skimming is "off book" fraud and cash larceny is "on book" fraud, in which funds are stolen after they are recorded in the company's accounts.

There are several ways fraudsters commit skimming fraud.

Cheque Skimming

In this scenario, someone intercepts an incoming check from a customer.

The employee steals the cheque and cashes it into their bank.

Since they're stealing these cheques before they have been recorded, an employee disguises their actions by hiding account statements and overdue notices.

REFUND SKIMMING

If a customer has overpaid, they should receive a refund.

A company with weak controls gives the fraudster an opportunity to pocket the refund check before it's been recorded in the Accounting system.

How Do They Do It?

Sometimes, the skimmer will go so far as to open up a bank account with a name that's very_close to the actual company's name. This makes it hard for anyone to notice the misspelling and uncover it.

For example, if the company's bank account name is "ABC renovations.", they might open up a bank account named "ABC Renos Inc.". In this scenario, the skimmer would likely be responsible for most of the account-related work, so, they can control it. This includes being the main contact for the customer and the main contact for billing and payment.

Fraudulent Write-Offs

This occurs when an accounts receivable employee credits a customer's account for a discount, a return, or some other form of a write-off. This technique can be used to cover up a previous theft or be used as a form of fraud. For example, let's say Nick has been keeping payment checks that were meant for the company to pay a bill owing from the customer... To hide his fraud, Nick will apply for discounts to hide the "missing" money.

As a form of fraud, an employee can also credit old or closed accounts with several discounts. This is usually uncovered during year-end.

This form of accounts receivable fraud is common in small businesses, where there's only one employee responsible for monitoring. An employee who doesn't share their duties with a colleague is less likely to get caught.

Fake Sales and Fictitious Accounts

Fake sales and fictitious accounts are typically set up to disguise one another. When someone makes a fake invoice, accounts receivable become inflated and there appears to be more money in the company. And at the end of the day, more money in the company benefits everyone in it. Once a sale has been entered, an entry is done to a payment that is never actually received, and eventually, this is written off. So, while the payment is never received, the effects and benefits that come from the false sale stay.

Company owners can create fictitious sales to make their business seem more profitable to banks. Commission-drawing sales staff might want to create false sales to meet monthly goals.

A receivables process with strong controls can help to expose or prevent this fraud.

The cost of Workers' Comp Fraud

A report by the Association of Certified Fraud Examiners (ACFE) concluded that businesses with fewer than 100 employees have the highest number of fraud cases.

Recently, an accounts receivable fraud scam tallied up more than $400 million in fake invoices. The story goes like this:

Oceanografia,a top service provider in the oil-related industry, would perform services and supply items for Pemex (the Mexican state oil company) and send them a bill. Pemex took a while to get around to paying the bills, so Oceanografia would send bills to Banamex (Bank of Mexico) instead. Banamex would pay the bill and wait to be paid back when Pemex had time. Eventually, Oceanografia stopped performing oil services but still sending bills to Banamex anyway. Banamex unknowingly paid fake invoices for years, extending millions of dollars in credit.

Preventing Accounts Receivable Fraud

Every business has a weakness and a really determined fraudster can scope this out with ease, but preventing accounts receivable fraud doesn't need to be that hard. Identify your weaknesses and fix them before it's too late.

Small to medium size companies are more susceptible to employee fraud than larger companies. In Canadian companies with fewer than 100 employees, the median loss for reported cases was $200,000, whereas, for companies with more than 100 employees, the median loss was only slightly less than $200,000.

According to the ACFE report, in 85% of cases, the fraudster displayed at least one red flag. In 50% of cases, the perpetrator exhibited multiple red flags. We will discuss red flags and the profile of fraudsters later in the book.

According to ACFE reports, tips are the most common means of detecting fraud, and anonymous hotlines are the best way to facilitate them. Other controls include surprise audits, anti-fraud policies, and employee support programs, which provide counseling to employees with personal problems that are affecting their work. A code of conduct, audits, and proactive data analysis are all associated with faster detection.

If you got through the last few pages without stopping for air, then I am impressed. You can see why employee based fraud can be so exhausting and frustrating.

Source: 2020 Report to the Nations. Copyright 2020 by the Association of Certified Fraud Examiners, Inc

[1] For this book and live presentations. I use only the 2020 reports as I felt the figures after this may be compromised due to COVID.

CHAPTER 3

THE 10-10-80 RULE

WHY DO EMPLOYEES STEAL?

10-10-80 RULE

I n earlier versions if this book, I had this buried in the content of the book somewhere. It is so important and can be a key turning point once a business understands it and puts things in place to protect itself.

According to many fraud experts, most organizations are operating within the 10-10-80 rule, meaning:

10% of employees will never steal no matter what

10% will steal at almost any given time, and

80% will go either way depending on how they view and rationalize their behaviour when an opportunity presents itself.

So, it seems that how effectively a company minimizes its risk of fraud is directly linked to its influence over this 80% group.

The one thing that comes to mind is having something in-house showing employees that this is being watched, it's on the radar using internal anti-fraud posters and having a meeting about it.

If there is an opportunity to steal, they will think twice when they see posters and it looks like everyone is on alert. The percentages speak for themselves. Fraud is waiting to happen and basically, the best way to combat fraud is to prevent it from happening.

It doesn't matter whether you're talking about a retail cashier swiping an extra dollar or two from the register or an accountant directing thousands of dollars into their personal account: if they're taking money—or anything else—from the business, it's considered theft or fraud.

SAMPLE ANTI FRAUD POSTER

WHY DO EMPLOYEES COMMIT THEFT OR FRAUD?

There is a wide variety of reasons employees would commit fraud and/or steal from companies that employ them. Some of the most common are:

1. FINANCIAL PRESSURES AND INCENTIVES

Employees who have money troubles in their personal lives are more likely to commit a crime by stealing. These could be because of high amounts of personal debt, irresponsible spending habits, and/or higher than needed cost-of-living bills.

2. OPPORTUNITY

The more access someone has, the more likely they are to feel they could potentially steal without being caught. Employees who handle thousands of units in a single day and know that some inevitably go missing may think that no one will notice if they take one or two units for themselves.

3. RATIONALIZATION

Sometimes an employee can convince themselves that their actions are justified for any number of reasons, including the size of the company, the presence of insurance that would cover the loss, a perception that their job performance entitles them to extra benefits or a belief that they deserve extra pay for being treated poorly or paid poorly.

PROFILE OF A FRAUDSTER/RED FLAGS

WHO THEY ARE AND HOW TO KNOW THE WARNING SIGNS

I have experience in this first-hand. I've been in the company of co-workers in different environments and saw them acting clearly different to each group of people they were speaking with. It may also depend on what they wanted to achieve or what they needed from them.

In my discussions with senior fraud/serious crime detectives over the years I have found that they have dealt with every type of criminal in their career. Some people, when they get caught, admit it, others try to fight it and use addiction as an excuse.

I've heard Detectives say that some fraudsters are the worst type of criminal that they have had to deal with and that some actually groom their potential targets and can act like a chameleon in many different scenarios to gain their trust and keep that trust.

In hindsight, I know now many of the warning signs were there. I just failed or chose not to see them.

~

One of the Fraud Detectives said that when they interviewed a certain Fraudster and questioned them about how their actions may have affected the families and employees involved there was no emotion. No movement at all. However, when they were discussing something like a vacation they were not going to be able to take from stolen funds or some money that they were not going to get because of the fraud being uncovered, that changed and there was a lot of motion, movement and twitching.

It is important to note that not all fraudsters are sociopathic or even at the level that we have been discussing. Sometimes, they steal because they feel they are put in a position where they have to make extra money in order to continue a certain lifestyle. Sometimes people just make bad decisions and it is never too late for forgiveness or redemption.

There were signs, there was even mention of things that in hindsight were red flags told to me by my wife. Things my wife saw and told me about at the time, that had made her feel uneasy.

She knew something wasn't right. Not only did I not listen to her or anyone else for that matter, but I also actually took exception and told them it was their problem, not the employees.

When it all came out I went through a roller coaster of emotions. I know it's not helpful to bash myself constantly. It's not my goal.

However, if we do not learn from our mistakes, we will be forced to repeat them.

∾

I should have listened to my wife.

∾

U sing the information that was presented in the <u>ACFE's Report to the Nations</u>, the following is a profile of a perpetrator, split out into different categories:

Position: Consistent with previous reports, the individuals most likely to commit fraud were in the "employee and manager" positions. Of the cases analyzed, 40.9% were employees and 36.8% were managers. The other significant category under position was the owner/executive, which made up 18.9% of the crimes.

Tenure: The report also analyzed data on how long the perpetrators were employed with an organization. In doing so, it was noted that losses were more significant the longer an individual worked for the organization. Employees with 1-5 years committed the most frauds at 42.4%. Those with 6-10 years at the organization came in at 26.5%, and those with more than 10 years were at 22.9%. This seems reasonable as one would assume the longer an employee is with an organization, the more responsibility they get, which in turn may give them more opportunity to commit the fraud.

Department: According to the Report, approximately 76% of frauds came from seven key departments: accounting, operations, sales, executive/upper management, customer service, purchasing, and finance. Of these, the accounting department had the most frauds at 16.6%. Coming in second, the Operations department made up 14.9% of the frauds, and in third, the Sales department was at 12.4%.

Gender: Of the 2,410 cases reviewed, 69% of fraud perpetrators were male and 31% were female. The Report noted that these percentages were consistent with previous studies which have found females to be responsible for between 30%-35% of frauds in every study since they began collecting data in 1996. Some of this distribution was attributed to the fact that men still make up a larger portion of the workforce than women, so it might be expected that their percentage would be higher.

Age: More than half (55%) of frauds were committed by individuals between the ages of 31 and 45. Less than 3% of crimes were committed by people over the age of 60.

Education Level: Coming in at 47.3%, perpetrators with a college degree were much more likely to commit fraud than someone without a degree. This category could be influenced by the fact that someone with a higher education level will most likely have a higher level of authority and have the opportunity to commit fraud more than someone who has a high school level of education, and much less authority and access within the organization.

Acting Alone or Colluding with Others: Are those committing fraud most likely to act alone or in collusion with others? The ACFE reported that 52.9% of cases involved only one perpetrator, which is down slightly from the 2014 Report (54.9%). The Report indicated that this decrease could be due to better anti-fraud controls related to separation of duties. However, if multiple individuals act together, they could still circumvent the system to commit the fraud.

Criminal History: The majority of occupational fraudsters are first time offenders. Only 5% of those committing occupational fraud were convicted of a prior fraud-related offence, and only 8% were previously fired for fraud-related conduct by a previous employer. These findings have been consistent since the ACFE's first report in 1996.

Employment History: Approximately 83% of individuals committing fraud had never been terminated or punished prior to the crimes included in the ACFE's Report. Some of this could be because some cases are never referred to law enforcement, offenders not receiving punishment, or entering into settlement agreements that are confidential. Therefore, this figure could be slightly inflated and the actual number of individuals with a history is higher.

Behavioural Red Flags

In addition to the specific demographic information identified in the Report, the ACFE also explored behavioural red flags that are common in fraud perpetrators. According to the ACFE, the following are the six most common red flags:

- **Living beyond means**
- **Financial difficulties**
- **Unusually close association with a vendor or customer**
- **Wheeler-dealer attitude**
- **Control issues, unwilling to share duties**
- **Divorce/family issues**
- **These six have been the most common red flags since this data was first tracked in 2008. The ACFE found that approximately 79% of perpetrators exhibited at least one of these six during their employment.**

Also, according to the ACFE study, 25 percent of internal fraud (theft in the workplace & fraud in the workplace issues) amounted to a loss of 1 million dollars on average

41% of employee-based fraud cases were done by employee-level staff, 35% were done at the manager-level, and 20% were perpetrated by executives

The study concluded that 75% of employees admitted to stealing from their employer at least once. Employee theft costs companies up to $50 billion annually

On average, 5% of an organization's revenue is lost to employee-based theft each year.

- 80% of fraudsters received some sort of punishment in response to theft.

Of this number, only 45% of owners and executives were terminated from their positions compared to 66% of managers and 76% of employees.

Behavioral Red Flags of Fraud

Recognizing the behavioral clues displayed by fraudsters can help organizations more effectively detect fraud and minimize their losses.

85% OF ALL FRAUDSTERS displayed at least one **BEHAVIORAL RED FLAG** while committing their crimes.

7 KEY WARNING SIGNS

42%
Living beyond means

26%
Financial difficulties

19%
Unusually close association with vendor customer

15%
Control issues, unwillingness to share duties

13%
Irritability, suspiciousness, or defensiveness

13%
Wheeler-dealer attitude

12%
Divorce family problems

LIVING BEYOND MEANS

Living beyond means

Financial difficulties

Unusually close association with vendor/customer

Control issues, unwillingness to share duties
Irritability, suspiciousness, or defensiveness
"Wheeler-dealer" attitude
Divorce/family problems

50% 40% 30% 20% 10%

'08 '10 '12 '14 '16 '18 '20

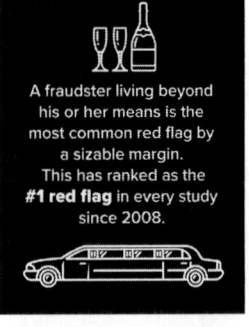

A fraudster living beyond his or her means is the most common red flag by a sizable margin. This has ranked as the **#1 red flag** in every study since 2008.

FIG RF-1 **Source:** 2020 Report to the Nations. Copyright 2020 by the Association of Certified Fraud Examiners, Inc.

CLASSIFYING RED FLAG BEHAVIORS

In **52%** of cases, the fraudster exhibited red flags connected to their **work duties.**

Unusually close association with vendor/customer
| 19% |

Control issues, unwillingness to share duties
| 15% |

Irritability, suspiciousness, or defensiveness
| 13% |

Wheeler-dealer" attitude
| 13% |

Complained about inadequate pay
| 8% |

Refusal to take vacations
| 7% |

Excessive pressure from within organization
| 7% |

Past employment-related problems
| 6% |

Complained about lack of authority
| 5% |

In **63%** of cases, the fraudster exhibited red flag behavior associated with his or her **personal life.**

Living beyond means
| 42% |

Financial difficulties
| 26% |

Divorce/family problems
| 12% |

Social isolation
| 9% |

Addiction problems
| 6% |

Past legal problems
| 5% |

Instability in life circumstances
| 4% |

Excessive family/peer pressure for success
| 4% |

JOB PERFORMANCE AS A WARNING SIGN

A fraud perpetrator's job performance will often suffer while the scheme is Each of these performance-related issues were cited in at least 10% of cases

13%
POOR PERFORMANCE EVALUATIONS

13%
EXCESSIVE ABSENTEEISM

12%
FEAR OF JOB LOSS

12%
EXCESSIVE TARDINESS

10%
DENIED RAISE OR PROMOTION

FIG RF-2 **Source:** 2020 Report to the Nations. Copyright 2020 by the Association of Certified Fraud Examiners, Inc.

~

AMERICAN EXPRESS AND COURTROOM DRAMA

Going back to Christmas of 2011, I was at home and I received a call from the American Express loss prevention department.

The call was about unusual activity on my American Express corporate card. They said we have a couple of charges that look highly unusual. There was plane tickets purchased online going to different destinations across the globe and I didn't remember anybody in the company needing to do that so we better look at the names on the plane tickets that they were purchasing. I definitely did not know or recognize the names so I suggested we lock the card to be safe.

The American Express representative then explained that the charges were not on my card, it's on one of the supplementary cards that a few employees are given. At that time, it could've been any of six people. It turned out to be our trusted employee.

It was their card, so Amex will still lock that card, but I told the representative that based on the charges being of a high value I would need the cardholder to review the entire statement and see if there's anything else on the statement that was fraudulent.

The American Express representative said that on Monday, I would need to review the statement with the supplementary card holder and then they will call Monday morning to review it and get this completed. On Monday morning I asked the cardholders to print out the latest Amex statement so we can review charges.

On Monday, the former employee presented me with an Amex statement a requested, and as expected there were charges for the plane tickets as well as telephone and Hi Speed internet charges that were legitimate. I checked off the few charges I recognized and questioned another for paper (that turned out to also be legitimate). I marked beside the suspicious charges the word "fraud", a check mark for the two I recognized and a question mark for another, meaning to just check it out further. American Express called at that moment to get me on the line, and I passed the phone call to the individual whose card it was. They came back into the room about half an hour later and let me know that the two plane tickets had been removed from our account and a new card would come in a few days.

NOTE: One the reasons I'm telling this is not to tell a story so much as to stress how much we need to look at our statements and deeply review the statements, even if somebody who is empowered in a position of trust were looking at them, we still need to have our eyes on it.

Fast forward almost 7 years later, and I am on the stand as a witness. I'm being cross examined for what seemed like the 13th or 14th day. The second to last piece of evidence was then put in front of me. It was a credit card bill.

I had testified that I did not look at the monthly statements. I trusted the individuals who had a company card and the fiduciary duty attached, to make sure they looked it over, and allocated the charges properly. What I mean by allocated obviously is if there's a Roger's phone bill, it was going to telephone charges. If it was a paper bill, it was going to office expenses, and so on.

So, this last piece of evidence was the same American Express bill I had looked at with the employee, and spoke with Amex about seven years earlier, and I didn't quite remember that right away.

The questioning went something like this "You say that you did not review any supplementary statements, however, in front of you is an American Express statement with your handwriting approving charges and questioning others.

At that moment, I was caught off guard and a little bit puzzled. I'm looking at it and I don't completely remember it. I didn't know exactly what it was, so they quickly withdrew the evidence and rested their case. I sat there completely stunned for about 5 seconds.

THEN IT HIT ME....

There were charges on those pages that they showed me. However, there were pages missing. Not only were pages missing, but areas of the pages I was shown seemed to be either altered, missing or redacted. Not redacted with black stripes or blocks, as is usually done, but almost like paper was covering up charges and it was photocopied. Now, keep in mind the evidence is no longer in front of me and the defence had rested.

When this hit me, it was so big of an AH-HA moment that I broke protocol and blurted out into the courtroom. "Excuse me, your honour, we need to bring that paperwork back. I just realized what it was, and it's critical that it comes back."

At first the judge was not game for that and the defence was protesting also. I told them that when the paperwork comes back and we show them what was in the statement, they will see that someone had willfully covered up areas of concern.

The judge allowed it, and I went through it pointing to areas where pages 1 to 4 were missing and we were only getting a part of page 5. I also pointed out how there were areas of the actual pages we did have that seemed to be redacted or whited out.

The judge then asked where we could get a copy of the actual statement to see what was being hidden and the Crown Attorney said he would bring it.

Sure enough, after lunch the Crown Attorney brought it back, and it had a $12,000 bracelet bought with the company Amex, an $11,000 cruise around the world, and many other personal charges. Probably the most shocking statement we have ever seen. So that kind of backfired on them.

I can't state this enough. The way to not have to go through this is to not let it happen.

CHAPTER 4
IT'S NOT YOUR ACCOUNTANTS FAULT

I n Chapter One I described how, when the fraud was first announced in the local newspapers there were three types of responses. One of them asked if we were going to sue our Accountants?

No, l am not.

Not only is it incorrect to think it's their fault it is the opposite. Our accounting firm did a great job. To be fair, people would ask how we all missed it and how the accounting firm did as well. We missed it because we weren't looking.

In our situation, the fraud is no one's fault but mine. I know it can happen to anyone..... I wasn't watching my business, I had poor control systems or none at all, and I didn't have the right people in place and I did not arm anyone with the power or the knowledge to look out for this for me and I gave somebody the power to control the narrative, the documentation, all the files and they were the main and only contact to our Accounting firm. They controlled the communication, the financials and also they reported to me. So they could pretty much do whatever they wanted.

Certified Accountants in Canada are part of a membership called the CPA. They are forward thinking and try to improve their members and keep them up to date with new laws and any changes all the time.

The task of an actual Fraud Auditor is to **gather evidence regarding a fraud**, which may also result in acting as an expert witness during legal proceedings. A fraud audit is actually a consulting service, rather than a type of audit, since the outcome does not involve giving an opinion on a client's financial statements or a statement to a bank or lender.

It is more specific than an audit because there's certain areas to look at and actions being inspected.

For typical Year-ends, Accountants both **verify the financial statements representing a business's bookkeeping throughout the year—** and prepare the final set of statements required to file that company's annual tax returns. They do this by following GAAP (Generally Accepted Accounting Principles). They do this with the information we give them and rely on that to be honest and truthful.

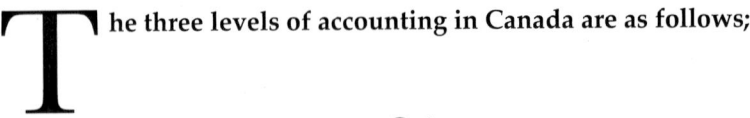

The three levels of accounting in Canada are as follows;

Notice to Reader

In this case, your accountant essentially takes the numbers you provide and generates a standardized financial statement, such as a balance sheet or income statement. The numbers are not reviewed for accuracy or to ensure that they are a true reflection of your business's activity. Instead, your accountant simply trusts that the numbers provided are correct.

A Notice to Reader is the most inexpensive way to have a financial statement prepared. Most small to mid sized companies are required to have this done.

Review Engagement

A Review is halfway between and Audit and a Notice to Reader and its name says it all. To prepare a Review, your accountant reviews all of the numbers provided before preparing a financial statement. They are looking for internal consistency, analyzing specific account balances and asking for explanations or further details if anything seems unusual or unreasonable. Reviews must follow Generally Accepted Accounting Principles (GAAP), and once completed must be signed by a public accountant. A Review instead of a Notice to Reader is usually necessary if your business is applying for a loan above a certain threshold.

Think of a Review as a 'light Audit.'

Audit

The most stringent of the three types of financial statements, an Audit is an extremely detailed process in which every single number is scrutinized and verified. An Audit also tests your financial reporting routines and practices. It also must follow GAAP, and once completed is verified by a public accountant who confirms that all of the numbers are fair and reasonable.

Because of this demanding process, Audits are highly trusted documents. Public companies are required to conduct annual Audits at year-end. Private companies typically only need to conduct an Audit if it's requested by a lender.

Don't just assume which level of financial statement your company needs. First ask yourself who will be using your statements, then talk to your accountant to figure out which financial statement is the best and most cost-effective.

~

How a Forensic Accountant Uncovers Fraud

An accountant doing regular statements, especially when the person committing the fraud controls what's given to him, has little chance of finding anything. However, the forensic accountant is another beast altogether. They are hired and have the training necessary to specifically seek out things like corruption or embezzling.

Forensic accountants are specially trained. Using tools of accounting, auditing, and investigative skills, forensic accountants can uncover crimes and can also testify as an expert witness.

Some techniques used by C.F.E's are:

Bank Account Analysis: The company's bank accounts can reveal details about the company's funds and cash flows. Do deposits accurately show receipts, loans and other payments? If not, where is it?

Investigation: If someone is misappropriating business assets, a forensic team looks for fictitious accounts, contracts, invoices, kickbacks, fake employee and/or vendors, personal expenses and expenses paid out that are not business related.

Inventory: Missing inventory can be a clue to schemes being perpetrated, and showing "lowered value" inventory and cost of goods can make a company appear more profitable. They look for how inventory is accounted and if there are any discrepancies.

It is important that we all understand our accountants different levels of liability and what they're being hired to do. Putting the job duties and scope of work in writing prior to engaging the accounting firm would be the best action.

CHAPTER 5
BALANCE SHEET BINGO
WHAT EVERY BUSINESS OWNER SHOULD KNOW ABOUT THE BALANCE SHEET

∼

"**W**ait a second……. You mean you want <u>ME </u>to present the financial evidence?"

∼

> *When they told me that I should be the one presenting the evidence on the stand, I was a little concerned. I would have to explain to the judge and everyone else in the court room, a very unorthodox and elaborate set of accounting movements that was designed specifically to hide fraudulent activity and confuse anyone looking.*

The trial date that we were preparing for was taking us into the seventh year of the case. We were concerned too much time had passed and the accounting staff that worked on the file may not recall everything, and that they are professionals who could talk slightly over our heads and in turn, the Judges and other court officials too.

There is not much worse than making a judge feel stupid or confused, and if the Defence smelled any weakness they may try to confuse the witness even further and frustrate and confuse the judge in doing so.

We decided that I should present the evidence......

Before I could do that, I needed to better understand how the balance sheet worked and how credits and debits worked within general journal entries. I also had to understand how entries may effect each other, keeping in mind that Judges, Crown Attorneys and support staff are not trained in accounting and bookkeeping.

My advice, Make sure that whoever testifies on the actual execution or mechanics of the fraud can do so with clarity and in terms that can be understood. Make it clear and concise. Keep it simple.

Balance sheet vs income statement: what's the difference?
I would always see Profit & Loss reports but generally the balance sheet was only brought up at year end.

Let's get down to the basics, the meat and potatoes.

The balance sheet and income statement (sometimes called profit and loss or P&L) are both important. What makes them different?

The income statement gives your company a picture of what the business performance has been during a given period, while the balance sheet gives you a snapshot of the company's assets and liabilities at a specific point in time. That is just one difference.

What is a Balance sheet?
The balance sheet is a snapshot of what the company both owns and owes at a moment in time. It is used alongside other important reports, such as the statement of cash flow

or income statements, to perform financial analysis. The purpose of a balance sheet is to show your company's net worth at a given time and to give the person reviewing it an insight into the company's financial position.

What is included in a balance sheet?
The balance sheet is a financial statement comprised of assets, liabilities, and equity at the end of an accounting period.

Assets
Assets include cash, inventory, and property. These items are typically placed in order of liquidity, meaning the assets that can be most easily converted into cash are placed at the top of the list. That makes sense.

Liabilities
Liabilities are a company's financial debts or obligations. They include things such as taxes, loans, wages and accounts payable.

Equity
Equity is the amount of money originally invested in the company as well as retained earnings minus any distributions made to shareholders/owners.
The foundation of the balance sheet lies in the accounting equation where assets equal liabilities plus equity on the other.

ssets = Liabilities + Equity

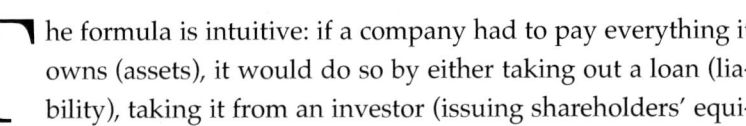

T he formula is intuitive: if a company had to pay everything it owns (assets), it would do so by either taking out a loan (liability), taking it from an investor (issuing shareholders' equity), or taking it from retained earnings.

The company's total assets need to equal total liabilities plus equity for the balance sheet to be considered "balanced."

The balance sheet shows how a company puts its assets to work and how those assets are financed based on the liabilities section. Since banks and investors analyze a company's balance sheet to see how a company is using its resources, it's important to make sure you are updating them every month.

What is an income statement?

The income statement, often called a profit and loss statement or P&L, shows a company's financial health over a specified time period. You can run a monthly or quarterly report.

It also provides a company with valuable information about revenue, sales, and expenses. These reports are used to make important decisions.

Both revenue and expenses are closely monitored since they are important in keeping costs under control while increasing revenue. For example, a company's revenue could be growing, but if expenses are growing faster than revenue, then the company could lose profit.

What's included in an Income Statement?

Income statements include revenue, costs of goods sold and operating expenses, along with the resulting net income or loss for that period.

An operating expense is an expense that a business regularly incurs.

These are expenses like payroll, rent, and non-capitalized assets or equipment.

Non-capitalized equipment is something you purchase that month or during the quarter, usually less costly than capitalized.

Capitalized assets or equipment appear on the Balance Sheet and they may be something like a commercial printer may buy for manufacturing, such as a larger production printer. You also see items in this area or schedule leasehold improvements. Larger based renovations are typically done this way also.

Capitalizing usually spreads the cost or depreciation over a three-year amortization on the balance sheet. Slowly depreciating it over time and it hits the financials 33% each year for 3 years instead of 100% in one year like non-capitalized assets.

A non-operating expense is unrelated to the main business operations, such as depreciation or interest charges. Similarly, operating revenue is revenue generated from primary business activities while non-operating revenue is revenue not relating to core business activities.

D o they have anything in common?

A lthough the income statement and balance sheet have many differences, there are some things that are the same. Along with the cash flow statement, they make up the three most important financial statements and even though they are used in different ways, they are both used by banks and potential investors when deciding on whether or not to be involved with the company.

While we know that the income statement and balance sheet are used to evaluate different information, we know both statements are critical when reviewing both the current and future financial health of a company.

In this next section, I want to just review something that confuses everybody, including me. Debits and Credits in accounting records and Journal Entries.

An easy way to start to understand journal entries is to think of the law of gravity, which says that for every action, there is an equal and opposite reaction. So, whenever a transaction occurs, there is at least two accounts that were affected in opposite ways.

Rules for Debit and Credit

First: **Debit** what comes in, **Credit** what goes out.

Second: **Debit** all expenses and losses, **Credit** all incomes and gains

Third: **Debit** the receiver, **Credit** the giver.

THE HIDDEN LOAN ACCT.

Now we come to the MAIN EVENT, or the reason why I feel it's important to drudge over the boring balance sheets, income statement, profit and loss reports, etc.

Below you will see an example of how someone can use the balance sheet to conceal ongoing fraud and, hopefully, if any of the dreaded debit and credit information has taken hold, you'll understand it.

First off, the employee created a bogus loan account on the balance sheet. They were also savvy enough (and had the access and credentials) to set the system to only allow this visibility to certain users. It was more of a clearing and holding account.

It takes a lot of time to manage something like this. There is a lot of moves because the person is trying to hide it during different moments in time, such as having a financial statement reviewed or year-end.

NOTE: In some accounting programs, top level users have the ability to run reports and use filters on them. The filters can even hide all the detailed activity and only show sub-total amounts. I remember clicking unhide and a cascade of ins and outs revealed themselves. I can only guess this was done to avoid anyone finding them at certain times (like accountants at year end or end of quarter).

I can only guess, but I feel the concept and execution of the way this was done may have come from what many owners do with deferred shareholder payments.

In a Corporation, if a shareholder has drawn $20,000 at the end of the fiscal year, that will show as a shareholders' loan on the balance sheet and that would need to be cleared with in a year on the financial statements. Cleared in this case, means paying it back or paying taxes on it. Paying it back would be the person writing a check for $20,000 to the company, and that amount is no longer on the balance sheet. Otherwise, the year wouldn't balance and the accountant at year-end would query this. Normally, they ask for a detailed report of that account to determine what it is and what has to be done.

It would be $20,000 out.

The other option is to move it to a payroll account and pay tax on it. I want to state here that this for a corporation and a shareholder might not be their first choice because you'd have to enter a lot more than 20,000 in order to gross 20,000. There are other methods and options to do this, however sometimes it may be the best choice depending on your situation. Declaring a dividend is one way, it is taxed at around 18% I believe. However, any other shareholder would have to draw the same in respect to their percentage of shares owned. So, based on $20,000, if someone had the same % of shares, they would also have to take $20,000. If they owned twice the amount if shares, then they would take $40,000. So, you see how it isn't optimal in multiple shareholder structures.

The way I see the similarity is when a shareholder defers it.

They take $20,000, and before year end repay it, and then right after year end they take it again. Not illegal, but frowned on after one year.

Because we had a fire, and some of the payroll remittances were delayed, we were remitting twice monthly and in larger amounts.

To summarize what was being done;

1) The employee would write handwritten cheques to themselves and deposit the cheques into their personal account.

2) The employee would also use multiple company credit cards for personal use.

3) The employee would at times buy assets and disguise them as business.

The checks, credit cards and expenses above have been taken out of the bank, so if nothing was done the bank would show it was out by the amounts taken.

American Express and Visa amounts the former employee used were entered in bulk form into a balance sheet account, not individually and separated by expenses most the time. I think they found it easier to avoid scrutiny by grossing up payroll and running them through when there were many transactions. The checks written are also entered individually and attached to that balance sheet account also.

To try to make this is as simple as possible, we mocked up and created a few that look a little like what the the original did. I will show one sheet of activity and one of the methods.

~

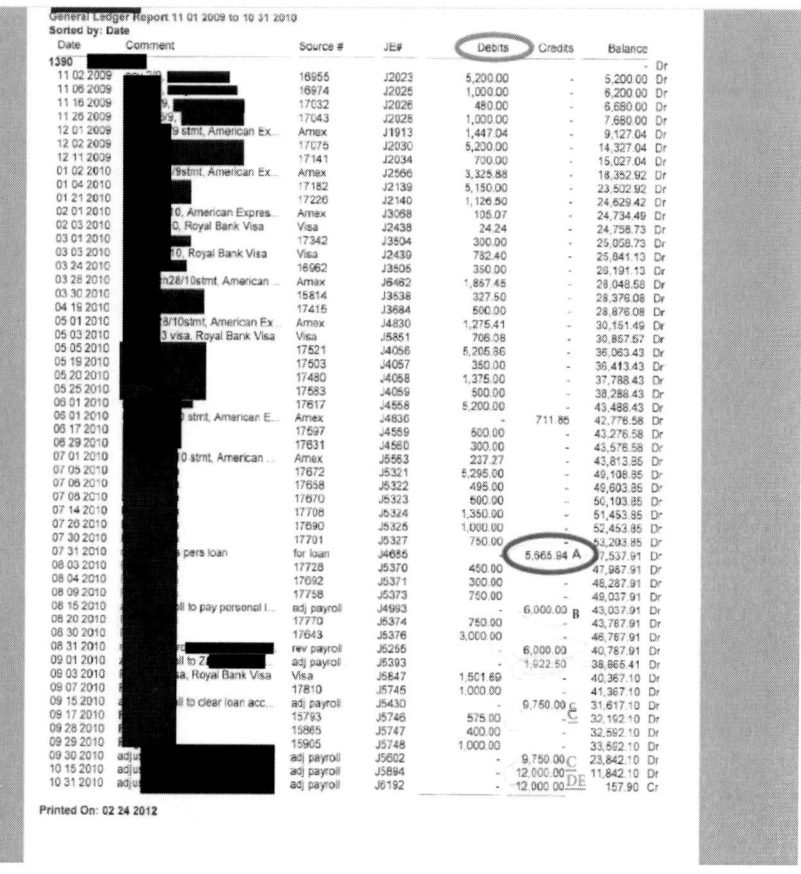

CHAPTER 4 BALANCE SHEET BINGO FIG-1-BS1

I n the first redacted image above. FIG-1-BS you will see a long list of transactions in the Debits column. All of these were personal and none were business related. It is just one sheet of probably dozens, and should give the reader an idea of the volume of theft that was occurring.

The second circled area is the transaction we will use as an example of $5665.94. These amounts were generally items grouped together (credit card charges grouped, or cheques). You will see that on this sheet, after that amount is credited/cleared you will notice that the fraudsters bogus account reduces. We can only guess that the amount chosen is one that they felt could be slipped through payroll without being discovered.

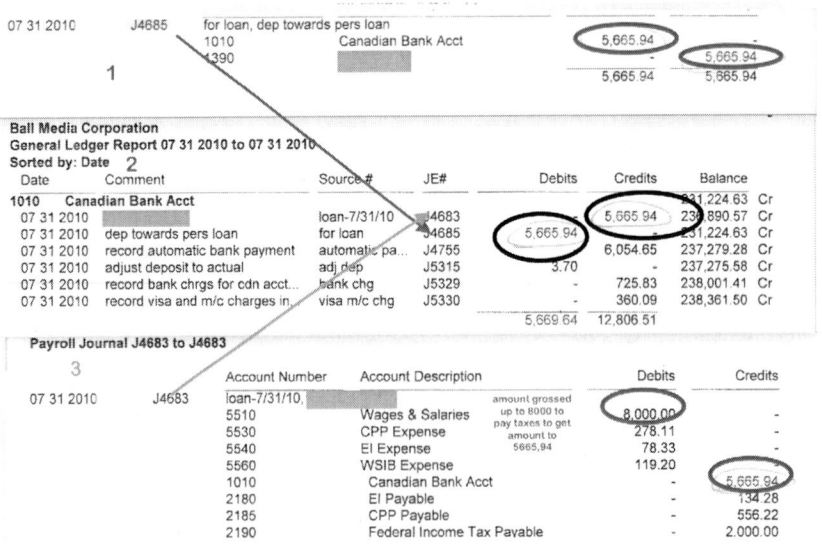

CHAPTER 4 BALANCE SHEET BINGO FIG-2-BS

#1: At the top of the sheet FIG-2-BS, you will see a lump sum amount of $5665.94 that was credited to the loan acct. and debiting to the bank (Journal #J4685)

#2 and #3: The amount was then recorded as a payroll entry totaling $8000.00 to wages and salaries, the wage entry would offset the bank and record an expense to wages. In order to do this the person would have to "gross" up the payroll entry to an amount that would result in the net amount being $5665.94, after taxes etc. were remitted ($8000.00).

That's right, the actual amount it cost the company for them to steal $5665.94 was about $8000.00 and they preferred the payroll method for clearing them out.

I want to point out here that this one transaction alone created all the moves I just explained. So if you look down that debits list I spoke of earlier, and just the one sheet that would need to be done with each one of them. So you could imagine the time spent to conceal and move over transactions.

Sometimes, it takes a while for all the pieces of the puzzle to make sense. Once I understood the crime itself and how it was executed, it allowed me to connect some other areas.

One would think, with all that going on with all those moves, certainly the individual would be nervous about somebody stumbling in and finding even just one of those many transactions that were fraudulent.

Keep in mind, the individual perpetrating the crime also controlled the documentation and the narrative.

Let's say somebody did happen to look at the records from that timeline and they found (for discussion purposes) a $10,000 payment to the employee. That would look a little suspect of course.

However, if we look at the employees actual payroll records, it would show zero payroll taken from January till October. On paper, it would seem that the company owed the employee $30-40,000 for not taking their attached payroll. Then in November the payroll that was not "taken" was entered manually and with General Journal entries.

CHAPTER 6

WHAT SHOULD I DO IF I UNCOVER A FRAUD?

What should I do if I uncover a fraud? I get asked this a lot.

What the victim does once they have uncovered fraud should be based on what outcome they are trying to achieve:

- 1 If the victim wants to try and recover their money, then starting a civil tracing process and a civil recovery lawsuit is what should be done first.
- 2 If the victim has decided to write-off the loss and they are interested in having the fraudster arrested and punished for the crime, then the victim should immediately report the fraud to police.
- 3 If the victim wants to recover their money and also wants the fraudster to be punished in Criminal Court, then it is necessary to coordinate these processes in the right order, so that the victim has the best chances of getting their money back.

Setting proper goals is one of the most important things a fraud victim will do at the forefront because it will assist in guiding the desired outcome.

Remember also, if the fraudster is put on notice that the fraud has been discovered too early, the chances of recovering the stolen money are greatly reduced.

Lets look at the anatomy of a criminal fraud case in Canada:

Let's look at the victims role.

- Victims communicate with the the arresting officer and the crown attorneys office.
- The victim is usually a key witness.
- Although there are actions and elements in place, the Criminal side does little to nothing to prevent the accused from moving money around or dissipating assets.
- This usually has to be done by your civil attorney.
- So, the victim pays civil retainer and fees with money they most likely do not have (as the money has been stolen), to recover or at least freeze money that's been stolen.
- If restitution is part of the judgment, it usually is a freestanding, which means there's no penalty for not repaying it, or no actions as a result of it.
- The victim needs to again engage in civil defence to collect it. Victims need to be careful here. I have heard cases where, because the victims money has been stolen, a civil firm comes on and agrees to be paid later. Then the victim may have no control of the billing and cannot decide to halt the civil trial because too much work has been done by the civil firm to not see it through. The victim needs to make decisions carefully, calmly and without too much emotion.

Choosing a civil attorney

I have been asked advice from victims of fraud not fewer than 25 times and in each instance the person does not follow the advice and most have admitted they should have.

The one piece of advice that most seem to disregard is the choosing of a civil attorney. After I ask the question: What is your end goal?

1. Put them in jail?
2. Recover the money?
3. Both?

Then I ask, have they hired a civil attorney yet? If they say "no" I ask, is there any reason why this needs to be rushed? There may be a pending property or something that needs to have a lien on it.

I suggest that they speak to a law firm that specializes in this. They will pay more her hour but they will get the answers they need quickly, and these firms are experienced in preparing criminal fraud complaints for the police and in bringing private prosecutions, as well as weighing the pros and cons of bringing simultaneous civil actions. There are new laws and findings all the time.

The lawyers at Investigation Counsel have what a victim needs. You may not like the answers but this is what you need to hear to avoid regret later.

https://investigationcounsel.com/contact/contact-us/

Most that don't hire civil firms, hire the people/firms that have done other areas for them and lack the experience, because fraud cases are not what they do.

CHAPTER 7

CRIME AND PUNISHMENT

SENTENCING, RESTITUTION AND FORFEITURE

This chapter has all the stats and numbers and looks formal but with the new precedences, the likelihood of people going to prison is low.

WHAT ARE THE LAWS AND WHO GETS THE TIME? STATS, STATS , STATS.

With any crime comes punishment, right? So, let's look at some of the data of the ACFE report on the response to fraud.

The report says 80% of perpetrators receive some punishment. Executives are less likely to receive punishment.

Internally

45% of executives are terminated, 66% of managers, 76% of employees

Civil litigation

28% of cases resulted in civil litigation

Of these cases: 41% resulted in a judgement for victims 36% settled

21% resulted in a judgement for the perpetrator

The median loss resulting in civil litigation is calculated at $400,000

Criminal prosecution

59% of cases were referred to law enforcement of these cases: 56% pleaded guilty / no contest

23% were convicted at trial

12% were declined prosecution

2% were acquitted

~

Source: 2020 Report to the Nations. Copyright 2020 by the Association of Certified Fraud Examiners.

I really don't want you to think I am going to stand on the soapbox and scream about how the legal system is broken or how the wheels of justice turn slow. We've heard all those things.

The truth of the matter is, I feel I have a right to an observation and opinion after being in multiple "Arenas" or courtrooms and seeing the Crown Attorneys, Judges, and other support staff. All of their work, including some of the changes, is a result of trying to make sure any citizen gets a fair trial.

I also know from being involved I can say confidently that all the people I dealt with wanted justice to be done and felt empathy for the victims.

I've heard people talk about the broken legal system and I've heard them say they don't care. I'm telling you with full certainty today that they do care, and that's from first-hand experience.

Every case is different, and every defendant is also different.

In a perfect world, things that greatly favour the accused would only be in place for people that actually want to defend themselves and clear their name.

The problem comes when they are bending over backwards to make sure somebody is not wrongfully convicted. What does that do for defendants in the Canadian criminal justice system that are trying to outlast, delay and frustrate?

There is a lot of discussions that have articles lately on the need for some sort of reform to the Canadian laws in regard to fraud. I feel we have to come up with better ideas, but I do not think the players on the prosecution side are doing anything wrong. In fact, they are just as frustrated as us at times.

 "We can't seem to open the files you sent... we don't have software to view the file... It's just not working when we get it home...

G AMES, SNAKES AND AUTOMOBILE

The defendants claimed they could not get the files from supplied counting records to open, they couldn't view any of the files when they brought them home, and they didn't realize it until the day before court.

The defence claimed they could not open the files. So... short of going to their house and opening it for them... which wasn't going to happen. As stated also prior, they then asked for all of the records to be printed out, knowing full well that is an unreasonable, and unachievable request. It was a game. Everyone knew it was a game, but nobody said it because they didn't want to challenge the defendants rights, so we could not print it out because that would be paper in the millions of sheets. We ended up putting it on one of the laptops, filmed with a video instruction and easy wind like instruction to get it open. They still claimed they could not open the files, so it delayed Court dates by months. That suited the defence well. Let me clarify another thing, this is not every case in the criminal justice system.

This is an example of defence trying to delay rather defend because, one would think, if they had something they wanted to find they would want to get into the files and get it sent so that they could be exonerated. The issue is all of us sitting on our hands knowing they're playing games unable to do a thing about it. When you think about what can be done, it's rather frustrating, because if the judges and crown attorneys just decline every request, and one of those requests turned out to be a wrongfully accused person it is defence, defender and that's that. Also, when to decide to stop pandering to a defence that's playing games and tactics. There would need to be guidelines, and I can't think of another way guidelines for something like this would not fall into being subjective. Every judge and every crown attorney may have a different view on what's what and when games should be stopped.

So I will just say as a victim, I felt like the crown attorneys and staff really cared but the system was not built for helping the victims, it seemed designed more for protecting the accused. There's no system in place for restitution to be accountable.
I will speak up about this a little, when the restitution order is handed out with a guilty conviction. It would be very helpful to the victims if there was some sort of punishment if the restitution is not made. I believe at the back of the book I included an article that had its focus on fine-in-lieu. It was a situation where the judge ordered a consecutive year sentence in a penitentiary for not repaying the money that was stolen within a certain timeframe.
It almost seems backwards. The only way plaintiffs who have had money stolen can get any non-dissipate orders or liens, is by using personal funds and engaging (paying for) a civil attorney.

They are using money to pay a civil attorney funds they may not have (because it was stolen) to execute a non-dissipate or similar order in civil actions.
Then when the plaintive gets money frozen, it's likely that the defence can put an order in to utilize that money for the trial. I couldn't imagine what that would feel like to have spent money I don't have on civil attorneys and successfully freezing cash for assets and then having the people who originally stole my money to be granted access to use it.

Then all I can think of is them still losing the case, but the money is now gone because the court released it to them to use.

Even if the plaintive doesn't have money frozen, the defence can still claim what's called a Rowbotham. It is where a defendant can demand the local town or city pay for their legal fees because they're impecunious (broke). In our trial specifically, the defence tried both avenues. It cost in the neighbourhood of $28,000 to stop and defend them from accessing funds that we had frozen. Then they proceeded with a Robotham application. As you can imagine, this takes time, so there was another eight month delay.

Right before the final trial the defence tried to subpoena all of the staff in the Crown attorneys office, this would eliminate all of them from being in the courtroom.

Games which caused another few weeks delay. There's too many variables to fix this. It would as I said, require subjectivity in opinion on whether somebody's playing a game or not.

So, please take this in. From someone who sat through this. I believe the only way to fight this is by eliminating the ability or reducing greatly the opportunity to execute a fraudulent act. I wish I could think of guidelines or even how that would start. Defence attorneys in fraud have possible defences listed right on their website. This can be done with integrating some of the processes in chapter 5 and putting an overall awareness into each company that this is real and happens all the time. We need to look out for it.

With recent decisions, I feel Canada is writing a book on how to get away with fraud.

What Is Fraud Under $5,000?

Similar to theft, $5,000 is a dividing line in fraud cases, splitting them into two categories. In Canada, fraud under $5,000 is a hybrid criminal offence that can be proceeded summarily or by indictment. If the Crown chooses to proceed summarily, you may not even have to appear in court, and can choose a fraud charge lawyer to represent you.

Many fraud cases under $5,000 in Toronto occur in retail or similar

settings known as shoplifting fraud. These include price manipulations, discount manipulations, fraud with credit cards, etc. Although
the value of such offences can be minimal, fraud under $5,000 is a
criminal offence in Canada and should always be taken seriously.

What Is the Possible Penalty For Fraud Under $5,000?

The maximum penalty for fraud under $5,000 is two years in
prison. Meanwhile, the severity of the punishment will depend on
whether the Crown will choose to proceed summarily or by indictment. The court will also account for the presence of aggravating
circumstances, such as premeditated planning, deception or breach of
trust.

If the Crown proceeds summarily, the maximum sentence is 6
months and/or a fine of up to $5,000. However, in indictment proceed-
ings the maximum penalty increases to 2 years. Meanwhile, in both
cases, criminal charges for fraud under $5,000 always come with a
criminal record, with different waiting periods before becoming
eligible for expungement.

The presence of a criminal record for fraud creates a stigma for
employment, finding a residence, and developing a social life. In addition, the court can impose an order prohibiting offenders from
obtaining or continuing employment, becoming a volunteer, or having
authority over real property or financial assets.

WHAT IS FRAUD OVER $5,000?

Fraud over $5,000 is known as "white-collar" crime, and is common in
such sectors as accounting, banking, or finance. Given the severity of
damages, this type of fraud is always treated as an indictable offence,
presuming the most severe sentences.

Examples of fraud over $5,000 include withholding material infor-
mation from potential investors, mortgage fraud, insurance fraud,
security fraud, and other similar cases. In addition, the Criminal Code
separately mentions cases of fraud where the total value exceeds one
million dollars, presuming an additional minimum mandatory
sentence.

. . .

What Is the Possible Penalty For Fraud Over $5,000? Those charged with fraud over $5,000 face grievous consequences, given its treatment in the Criminal Code. These consequences have become more severe after amendments instituted in November of 2012, which excluded fraud over $5,000 from eligibility for conditional sentences. Unlike sentences for less serious offences, which can be served under house arrest, the penalty for fraud over $5,000 presumes prison time for the total sentence period.

Therefore, anyone charged with fraud exceeding $5,000 faces a maximum sentence of up to 14 years in prison. In addition, fraud cases over one million dollars include a mandatory minimum sentence of two years.

Both frauds under $5,000 and over $5,000 are criminal offences that are fraught with serious penalties, including prison time, prohibition orders, and the stigma of a criminal record. Meanwhile, fraud over $5,000 comes with a maximum penalty of 14 years without the eligibility for conditional release.

Introduction and Brief description

Fraud is the wrongful or criminal deception intended to result in financial or personal gain. The definition of Fraud is left ambiguous in order to capture the vast nature that these offences occur. There are many examples of Fraud, but most commonly seen are Telemarketing scams, online scams, Identity Theft and Business scams.

SECTION WORDING

380(1) Every one who, by deceit, falsehood or other fraudulent means, whether or not it is a false pretence within the meaning of this Act, defrauds the public or any person, whether ascertained or not, of any property, money or valuable security or any service, (a) is guilty of an indictable offence and liable to a term of imprisonment not exceeding fourteen years, where the subject-matter of the offence is a testamentary instrument or the value of the subject-matter of the offence exceeds five thousand dollars; or (b) is guilty (i) of an indictable offence and is liable to imprisonment for a term not exceeding two years, or (ii) of an offence punishable on summary conviction, where the value of the subject-matter of the offence does not exceed five thousand dollars.

COMMENTARY

In R. v. Olan et al., the Supreme Court of Canada established a definition of fraud that included elements of "dishonesty" and "deprivation". In R. v. Stewart, the Supreme Court of Canada ruled that deprivation of confidential information, in the nature of a trade secret or copyrighted material that has commercial value, is to be considered within the scope of fraud. In 2004, section 380(1)(a) was amended to increase the maximum penalty from 10 to 14 years. In 2011, section 380(1.1) was added to include a mandatory minimum sentence of 2 years incarceration for offences over $1 million.

A MANDATORY MINIMUM PUNISHMENT FOR FRAUD?

The punishment for Fraud is set out within this section. As of 2011, mandatory minimum sentences may apply, if the total amount determined to be lost is over $1 million then the mandatory minimum is 2 years.

I have already talked about how punishment/sentencing can range from house arrest all the way up to several years in prison, depending on the size and complexity of the crime or if there is remorse, or if they are a first time offender. What about restitution orders, asset forfeiture and fines?

In very rare cases where a convicted fraudster has paid the money back prior to the case before sentencing, this will usually result in a lower sentence.

The Crown and the judges are supposed to take steps to ensure victims in these crimes get paid back.

The above has not been my experience in the court system. If I am being honest, I have seen more cases given a summary judgement and even heard crown attorneys tell victims to chase after the fraudster in civil courts.

Technically there are three different types of orders designed to assist victims collecting under the Criminal Code:

Restitution

Restitution orders are in place to allow the courts an option to order a convicted person to pay back the victim of fraud.

Section 738 of the Criminal Code says that judges are also permitted to make up to the full amount of any property that was lost as a result of the fraud. The judge should set out a timeline for repayment.

It clearly states that the accused's inability to pay does not prevent a restitution order from coming forward under the Code.

However, the courts have held that judges are allowed to take into account the fact that an accused person cannot pay the order in deciding whether restitution is appropriate, or how much restitution to order.

In a 2010 decision, the Ontario Court of Appeal explained the objectives restitution orders are intended to fulfill, which judges are supposed to consider when deciding whether to make a restitution order. The Court stated that the judge needs to consider the nature of the offence, whether a breach of trust was involved, and the impact that a restitution order would have on an accused's prospects for rehabilitation.

What if a restitution order isn't repaid?

Section 741(1) of the Criminal Code says that if a restitution order made by the court is not repaid the person who is owed the restitution can file the restitution order in any civil court in Canada, and the restitution order will become enforceable against the offender in the same way it would be if it was a judgment in a civil proceeding.

In other words, the person who is owed can go into a civil court and turn the restitution order into a civil judgment, and can then seek to try to get the money that way. This would allow things like a wage garnishment or a writ of seizure and sale of property.

This is where I have a problem. It's good that the restitution order exists, however, restitution orders have to be enforced in civil courts if they are not paid back. That is time consuming and frustrating.

It's very important for me to state that the code does not have any further punishment if the money is not paid back. So, there's no incentive for the fraudster to pay it back. The code does not set out any further punishment if the restitution order is not paid back.

Forfeiture orders

The courts also have the power to order a convicted person to forfeit money or property upon conviction of an offence.

There are two different ways these orders can be made. The first is a forfeiture order for the "proceeds of crime". Section 462.37 of the Code sets out a procedure that allows the Crown to apply to a court to seek forfeiture of "proceeds of crime". Here's my experience with this, it's very difficult because the detectives involved with the crown have to show a direct correlation to the money that was stolen and the money that was used to buy a property or is in a bank account. Most fraudsters move their money around, it's not that easy to trace, if not impossible.

The second way to seek forfeiture of money or property is set out under section 490.1 of the Criminal Code and applies to "offence-related property." I won't bore you with any details on this one. Basically, if you committed a crime in the property the crown might be able to request an order to seize and sell. This one has no teeth and is easily fought. Not to say it hasn't happened, but not very often.

Fines

In cases where fraud has occurred but the "property" obtained by the offence cannot be located or has been transferred to a third party, section 462.37(3) of the Criminal Code allows the Crown to apply for a "fine-in-lieu of forfeiture." The convicted fraudsters ability to pay does not matter here, even if they don't have the money the court will impose the fine anyway, so long as the Crown has been able to demonstrate the value of the property that was obtained as proceeds of crime that haven't been recovered.

Now I personally feel this next part is a great deterrent for fraud. Somebody who doesn't pay back $500,000 is looking at 4 years in a penitentiary. They make you think twice about committing a crime, and if you did commit crimes, paying it back as well. However, Judges rarely hand out any terms with discretion.

The Code also sets out jail sentences that must be imposed if the fine is not paid back. The amount of jail time that is supposed to be imposed increases depending on how large the unpaid fine is: The imprisonment mandated for failure to pay a fine in lieu of forfeiture is substantial, and can often exceed the prison sentence that was imposed for actually committing the fraudulent offence. In 2021 the Ontario Court of Appeal dismissed a claim that these mandatory punishments were excessively harsh and a violation of the Charter of Rights and Freedoms.

The reality is that the fines imposed by the courts can often involve huge sums of money, and that accused people may not be able to pay them back in time. Although the Criminal Code sets out mandatory jail terms that follow a refusal to pay back a fine, there are still things that can be done to avoid having to serve time in jail. When a fine isn't paid back in time, the court issues a "warrant of committal" that requires the accused to serve the jail sentence set out by the Criminal Code. However, the Court has the power under section 734.3 of the Criminal Code to vary the term of the order and to give an accused person a longer amount of time to pay the money back.

In addition, section 734.7 (1) of the Code provides that a warrant of committal should only be issued where the court is convinced that the accused has "refused" to pay the fine "without reasonable excuse". The courts have held that this means a court cannot issue a warrant of committal where an accused has a "reasonable excuse" for not paying the fine, and the courts have also held that an inability to pay the fine is a reasonable excuse. This means that even if the time for paying back the fine expires, an accused person can still demonstrate that the reason the fine hasn't been paid back is that they don't have the money and can't afford it. The courts have suggested that being too poor to pay the fine back, in other words, is not a reason to send someone to jail.

Instead, the court at the committal stage will be looking for more than an inability to pay back the fine. The warrant of committal will only issue where there is a refusal to pay the fine, and where there is no reasonable excuse for the refusal.

CHAPTER 8
RECOVERY
WRITS, GARNISHMENTS, ENFORCEMENT AND LIENS

As I discussed earlier in the book, I had many assumptions and pre-conceived ideas about what would be done to assure defendants do not start liquidating assets before the trial begins. Sometimes a judge will issue a non-dissipation order. These are more common in matrimonial cases. This is usually also set in place prior to a trial taking place. I can say, its been 12 years and I am still muddling through trying to get the lot we have/had frozen.

The decision at some point comes down to this. Do you want to put the perpetrators behind bars or do you want to recover money? You can rarely have both and sometimes neither.

To recover any funds, you need to act in the civil realm and retain and pay for a civil lawyer. The criminal and civil actions rarely have any connection to each other. However, the civil case in order to even be able to collect any funds, that's assuming there is some, need to rely on guilty verdicts, restitution orders and terms of any restitution as well as any other sentencing or non-dissipate actions that the criminal court may hand out.

"It has to go before the Courts"

A little advice: Whenever you hear this on the civil side, it means that paperwork needs to be generated and either a motion or affidavit needs to be created, and it generally costs you money. Be careful. Someone may need a new car....

When looking at a land registry, they call liens and non-dissipates etc. Instruments. Most start with letters such as NK before the numbering and will identify what the items are. They are usually Court appointed, but to be honest most lawyers and some title search professionals have access to create and extend any of these Instruments at will. So, one needs to be careful when viewing and questioning all of it.

E nforcement Methods
You would think that once you have a courts decision or order it should be easy. Enforcing these methods can be time consuming and costly. There are basically four methods to enforce a civil judgment for the payment or recovery of money in Canada, and specifically in Ontario:
- a writ of seizure and sale;
- garnishment under the Rules;
- a writ of sequestration under the Rules; and
- the appointment of a receiver.

Sheriffs sale : A creditor request and/or require the assistance of the sheriff to enforce a domestic judgment for the payment of money. The creditor will need to file a writ of seizure and sale with the sheriff and move to enforce the writ after filing. As a practice note, depending on the nature of the defendant (eg, financial institutions being reliably willing to satisfy judgments voluntarily), moving to enforce a writ of seizure and sale should be done promptly after obtaining judgment, unless assets have been frozen prior to judgment. The creditor must provide the sheriff with a direction to enforce, which includes detailed information as to the amount of the order, the amount and date of any payment, the rate of post-judgment interest and the costs of enforcement.

Upon receipt of the direction to enforce a writ of seizure and sale, the debtor's property can be seized. The Execution Act empowers the sheriff to use reasonable force to enter the debtor's land and premises if the sheriff has reasonable and probable grounds to believe that there is valuable property on the land or premises. One exception to this power is that the sheriff may not enter a dwelling with force unless a court order is obtained.

There are exceptions to the types of personal property that can be seized. For example, household furniture, utensils, equipment, food and fuel contained in the debtor's permanent home, up to a prescribed value, is not seizable, and neither are pension entitlements.

The sheriff can enforce a writ against personal or real property. The writ will be valid for six years from the date of the judgment, but can be renewed. A writ will give the debtor priority over other unsecured creditors, but that priority is lost if the debtor becomes bankrupt. Other creditors who have perfected security interests in the debtor's property will also have priority.

Before the sheriff sells personal or real property that was seized pursuant to a writ, notice must be provided to the creditor of the time and place of the sale. At the time of print, the fee to begin a Sheriffs sale was $10,000.00

Mareva injunctions

The remedy of a Mareva injunction is so named having adopted the name of the plaintiff company in a 1975 English Court of Appeal decision (*Mareva Compania Naviera SA v. International Bulkcarriers SA*). Such an order prohibits the dissipation of the defendant's assets. In effect, it provides a form of pre-judgment execution and has the effect of freezing a defendant's assets so they cannot be disposed of or transferred pending the outcome of the litigation. As a result, it is a difficult remedy to obtain and is a rare and extraordinary order.

A Mareva injunction is most often awarded on a shorter term (ten-day) temporary basis and then extended or usually denied at the actual hearing.

Only in Exceptional Circumstances

The process to obtain a Mareva injunction is difficult for the plaintiff. These orders in their nature, will prejudice the defendant. They seem like a temporary short term fix only, possibly in the beginning of a trial.

Execution of writs

What is an execution? Executions arise in the context of a lawsuit, after the successful party (the "judgment creditor") obtains judgment against the other party (the "judgment debtor"). The judgment creditor can obtain a writ and file it against the judgment debtor.

In Ontario, the term "writ of execution" includes the following: a writ of seizure and sale, a writ of seizure and sale of land, a writ of seizure and sale of personal property, a writ of sequestration, a subsequent writ that may issue for giving effect to a writ listed in any of clauses an order for seizure and sale of personal property, real property or both real property and personal property, and any other process of execution issued out of the Superior Court of Justice or the Ontario Court of Justice having jurisdiction to grant and issue warrants or processes of execution.

A judgment creditor may file a writ of seizure and sale of land in any county or district where the judgment debtor owns land. The writ will encumber any land presently owned or land which may be purchased in the future by the debtor in the county(s) or district(s) where the writ was filed. If the judgment creditor wishes to enforce a writ in 2 multiple locations, separate writs must be filed in each place. The above is all the more proof that you need to avoid fraud at all costs, stop it before it happens or you could get stuck in the endless loop of the paperwork and process.

MY FINAL THOUGHTS

So, in the end, the thing I cannot stress enough is that we need to make sure we put actions and elements in place to catch, hinder and stop fraud, because as I have said, once you are in, there is no easy way out.

I am certain that this book will have many revisions being that it is my first. I am finding things to change every time I read it. I am happy we added the Real World Examples. I really feel that it is one of the most interesting sections because it shows real world examples of what is happening in the courts and how victims are affected in the real world. You're seeing how certain cases are defining the way criminals are getting away with fraud and others, even murder, with the Jordan B11 bill.

You also see how it seems that the victims aren't considered in a lot of the judgements and the way restitution orders are placed. When you are 5 years into a case and trial or 3rd trial and you get the realization that you are trapped, the only way out would mean giving in and allowing it to happen. It would mean as memories fade, people may say to your family, "Well, it never got resolved I guess"?

The comments on criminal restitution orders being more fiction than substance is so well stated. It is so correct. I can say that, because I was dragged in and out of multiple court rooms. For over a decade. At first thinking we would be considered and then just hoping that we would be considered, and at the end I was not expecting to be considered. We were only spectators and our losses will never be validated. Not to mention the intangible opportunity, costs, and years and years of momentum that was abandoned.

I will say the Crown Attorneys office and staff never gave in and never gave up and they could have.

As I write this it is 2023. In two months it will be over 11 years and we still haven't gained access to the property we were able to get a non-dissipate order on. We did however pay their tax bill on that property. Yes you read that correctly, we pay a tax bill that was overdue on the property. The same property that we paid our civil attorneys to get a non-dissipate order on.

If terms of sentencing, if there had been a fine-in-lieu attached, at least there would be incentive for someone to repay.

I know if I thought I was going to get an extra four to six years of penitentiary time if I don't pay back the money stolen, I may think twice about stealing that money. I may really try to repay it also.

However, if I were reading the article where the woman stole $1 million from the bank, that outcome actually seems quite enticing to me and to be honest, not that much work for $1 million.

The fact that the bank was admonished and the casino was berated isn't surprising, just disappointing. I have to ask if the victim was a smaller operation and not a Billion Dollar Bank, would the outcome have been the same? I can only guess the bank doesn't want to lose money any more than a smaller company does, but did the bank just want to get it behind them and cut off the bad press?

These businesses do their best to deal with addictions and shortcomings. However, in the end it's not their fault. Blaming the workplace or the bar or casino? That's a cop-out. Trusting that the fraudster was telling the truth about going to the boss for help. Also, what was the boss going to do? Give her time off and pay for addiction counseling? I felt the fraudster left with warm and fuzzies, oh yeah, and $1 million! We wouldn't of known she was stealing $1 million by the tone of the proceedings and the article other than having read it earlier.

I was shocked and exasperated when I read the end of that $1 million banking fraud trial and the judge said to the fraudster I wish you the best of luck, but was angry with the casino and the bank. As I said, I know the individuals in these cases are dedicated to justice and serving the victims.

Is it because they don't feel the pain and the loss that the victims do? They've been in it too long perhaps? The restitution order is hollow and offers the victims no real chance of recovery whatsoever. The fact that $1 million may be a rounding error to the bank doesn't matter! What if it was a smaller mom and pop store locally.

In some of the articles I have added, I realize that the cases have nothing to do with fraud but I felt they would give the reader a clear idea of what the Jordan rule is. How it affects families. Not just families of fraud victims but also families of murder victims where criminals got to go free because of loopholes in the Canadian justice system not moving cases fast enough for them.

I want to comment and reiterate something in one article that hit a nerve with me. It was in the article entitled "Man defrauds own family, friends. I have copied it again below.

How the victim states I don't really care what they do to him or how they deal with him, I want my money back. In the end I believe that's the victim realizing the courts are going to do nothing about it even if you spend your own money civilly. The way Groot explains how many factors initially want the fraudster to be punished and they come to realize the criminal justice system is a high stakes game. I can relate to that, I was there, outside of a court room for what seemed like the hundredth time. Broke and exhausted. Feeling like nothing that happened to us mattered in the end. That is one of the reasons why I wanted to speak to people, and write this book.

The only way to truly avoid these things, is to put oversight and systems in place to prevent it from happening because the journey to get justice, if at all, is long and comes with no guarantees.

People are giving up pursuing justice through the criminal justice system at times because they realize the outcome doesn't really benefit them. The only catch is, pursuing only through the civil system is costly. At $300-$500 an hour for a good civil attorney, someone who is already lost hundreds of thousands of dollars potentially may not have the resources to spend another $200,000-$300,000 on lawyers.

In response to frustration with the criminal process, once of the victims was quoted as saying: "Quite frankly, I really don't care what they do to him and how they deal with him. I need my money back. I want my money back." Ultimately this is where we find most fraud victims end up. While many fraud victims initially want the fraudster to be punished, they come to realize that the criminal justice system is a high stakes game – where Judges (who are funded by taxpayers), complain about the government-run Courts and Crown prosecutors (who are also funded by the public) as living in a culture of complacency, while fraud victims see the government and the Courts living in a culture focused on the Charter rights of the accused as if they are some holy grail at the expense of their own rights to justice. To state otherwise, while the Courts cloak themselves in the comfort that the Charter is the ultimate law in the country, this does not resonate well with victims who have no "right" they can point to in the Charter to ensure their criminal complaint is fairly dealt with on the merits. It is because of decisions like Jordan that fraud victims ultimately give up on pursuing justice through the criminal system.....

I pointed out many games and tricks fraudsters use to delay and frustrate court rooms. Weeks of costly delays and endless administration costs and time to rebook and organize dates. Many of the tactics are obvious and no one says a word because they are concerned about infringing on the rights of the accused.

Instead of allowing all this, institute a process not unlike the NFL has when Officials cannot make the call confidently themselves, they go to instant replay and have another mediating judge or group of judges make the call instead of breaking for 3 weeks and paying all the officials and court employees to do so, when an accused tries to Subpoena the entire courtroom of professionals so they can't have a trial. Something everyone knows is complete nonsense. The Judge is able to call in a court appointed Mediator to decide if the subpoena of an entire Crown attorneys office is needed or if the defence truly cannot open the accounting files. This would save time and money.

In the end, if anything I say here helps anyone gain one more valuable day back in this life with your families, one more nights sleep, one more time that someone can feel proud of the company they own and one more time they feel their families are safe financially again it's all worth it. Be engaged, review your financials, put oversights in place, put checks and balances in place. Small things, but it will be a better life in the end.

Thank you.

John Ball

REAL WORLD CASE EXAMPLES
ARTICLES, BLOGS AND OPINIONS

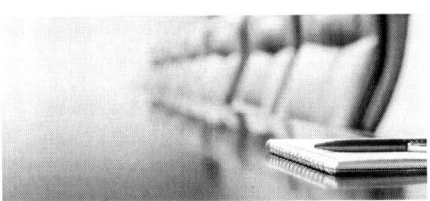

I have gathered some articles of interest that showcase discussions and blogs from some very reliable sources. The canadianfraudnews.com and investigativecounsel.com mostly.

In my opinion, these two above sources for news and developments along with the ACFE reports for stats is all anyone needs.

I have truncated the articles in places to help get to the point a little faster. I urge you to read the full articles if you wish.

I say this a lot but in Canada, we are writing the "How to Get Away with Fraud Hand-Book" for would be fraudsters and Defence Attorneys that need tools to get the clients off.

I've redacted information in some places. I feel it gets too close to someone related, or close to home.

This article shows how the people working within the system are really trying to do the right thing, but in the end, I think just contributing to the get-out-of-jail-free fraudster playbook.

On one side, I see them seemingly trying to help someone rehabilitate themselves, yet on the other side, I see everybody getting blamed for this except the person who committed the fraud of $1 million.

Why on earth should we trust the word of someone who stole a Million dollars? The fact that the court believed that she talked to her supervisor about the gambling issue is astounding. It still shouldn't take away from the fact that she stole 1 Million dollars!

I have full confidence that the judge and the Crown Attorneys in this case are doing the best that they can do for the community. The fact that the victim was admonished for not helping her is unsettling to me… That is if she actually did ask for help. I have a hard time getting my head around this one.

Addicted gambler gets house arrest after stealing $1 million

A woman who stole almost $1 million from her Bank-employer was given a remarkably light sentence in Ontario Court last week due to her equally remarkable response to the crimes.

xxxxxxx, 56, was sentenced to a form of house arrest for two years rather than being sent to jail, which is typical for frauds of that magnitude.

"When I first received this file I screened it for a penitentiary sentence," admitted assistant Crown attorney, xxxxxxx xxxxxxx sentencing hearing.

But through discussions, the Crown's office came to agree with xxxxxxs defence lawyer, xxxxxxxx, that the woman was already doing everything in her power to rehabilitate herself.

xxxxx's story began when she and co-workers from the xxxxx branch celebrated a birthday at the xxxxx Casino.

It started a major gambling addiction for the woman as she returned repeatedly to the casino, eventually spending $100,000 of her own funds.

xxxxx said xxxxxxx went to her employer seeking help for her addiction but was given short-shifts and offered no counseling.

According to police, she then began using her bank position to transfer money between client accounts and open new accounts in the names of some clients.

Her scheme worked from October 2010 until November 2014, when an internal bank audit uncovered the theft.

By that time, the bank had lost nearly $1 million, although it ensured no clients were out of pocket. The bank wasn't initially named because it insisted, as the victim of a crime, it didn't want to be identified.

She wasn't charged until February 2016 and by that time, despondent at what she had done, she tried to take her own life.

With family help, the court was told, she opted for redemption. She got into a residential addiction facility, started attending Gamblers

Anonymous, and saw medical doctors, a psychiatrist, a psychologist, and an addictions counsellor.

Her addiction was a mental illness," said the lawyer xxxxx. "She sought help from her superiors and didn't get it and was driven to such desperate straight she was ready to kill herself."

Now, she has done "everything in her power to try and fix this."

The defender and prosecutor agreed that she should face an extended sentence of house arrest and a free-standing restitution order in favour of the bank should she ever come into money.

Justice xxxx aid xxxxx had been extremely proactive about her rehabilitation. She has performed community service and moved to her father-in-law's xxxx area farm where she milks cows, goes to church, counseling, and doctors' appointments, and cuts grass at three farms.

The judge asked each lawyer to justify the jail-free sentence to an imaginary member of the public and then said he wanted to address the "elephant in the room"–the similar and highly publicized fraud case which has been wending its way through the justice system for five-and-a-half years.

She stole almost $1 million from her employer and isn't going to jail. The other case has been found guilty of stealing $500,000 from her former employer and you are seeking a penitentiary term of three years.

"The difference is substantial," explained xxxxx.

She took immediate responsibility, admitted everything to the police, retained counsel, and took steps to deal with her addiction issues. The other offender is still expressing no remorse."

He added that she blames no one but herself while evidence in his other case shows that the case in question has blamed the system, the police, the Crown's office, and the victims while denying all responsibility for her actions.

"And she was addicted before she took any money from the bank," "Addiction, whether it's crack cocaine, Fentanyl, alcohol, or gambling, changes the whole nature of an individual's wiring."

The judge noted she saved the taxpayers the expense of a long, expensive fraud trial.

She expressed her shame to the judge, saying she thinks about what she did to her employer each day.

"I take full responsibility for what I've done and I will accept any sentence and use it to benefit my life."

She said she's been treated for depression and anxiety and now has an excellent support system for doctors and counsellors.

"I do my twice daily barn work and I'm working hard to be a better person, wife, and grandma. It may not be enough for what I've done, but it's all I have."

The judge had harsh words for the xxxxxx casino which "had to have known she was coming in," at times twice a day, every day, and losing considerable sums of money.

"I have an element of rage for a casino that allows that," "The eye in the sky at the casino had to know and yet this was allowed."

The judge said her case was the more common fallout of legalized gambling than the community's previous worries about crime mobs and prostitution.

An OLG spokesperson responded after the sentence that, like all Ontario casinos, xxxxxx has responsible gambling features that include training front-line workers to watch for red flag behavior, self-exclusion programs, and responsible gambling resource centers.

"There are more than 100 locations across the province where Ontarians can access free counseling and other problem gambling support services," he said.

A bank spokesperson said the bank wasn't in a position to comment on the sentence.

A house arrest confines her for two years to the three xxxx area farms where she's working. She's allowed to go to church, counseling, and medical appointments as well as a once-a-week afternoon to get groceries and run errands.

She has to stay away from all bank branches and casinos, and avoid all online gambling, and complete 120 hours of community service.

"This case is what can happen when people take ownership of what they've done and correct their behavior," said the judge.

"Good luck – and I mean that."

Ok, I am going to just say it. What a complete sad day for victims and justice…. Good Luck? She doesn't need luck, she has a Million bucks.

∾

Taken from canadianfraudnews.com

∾

Fine-in-lieu-of-forfeiture

In the second case, this is an example of one of the laws in Canada that could help deter fraudsters. In this article, you'll see that the individual that committed fraud had a time frame that was part of the sentencing to pay the restitution. If he didn't, then he would have to face 6 consecutive years in the penitentiary. So the victim getting paid back seemed to be a consideration.

This is rare, it was talked about while I was involved in a case but never came to fruition. I feel that these laws need to be in place to look after the victims. So, the judgment can have what I call "teeth" and consider the victims in this also. I know this will deter people from actually committing fraud if they know they may face six years in the penitentiary if they do not pay back the money.

(This is truncated) In 2016, V was convicted of fraud and theft of maple syrup. The stolen maple syrup had a large market value. He was given jail time as well as a restitution order which had terms attached to it and a punishment.

If he didn't repay it in a certain amount of time, he would go away for another 6 years.

The trial judge imposed a fine on V in lieu of an order for forfeiture of property that was proceeds of crime ("fine-in-lieu").

Mr. V has 10 years to pay this fine, in default of which he is subject to imprisonment for 6 years consecutive to any other term of imprisonment."

Taken from website supremeadvocacy.ca

Right to a Trial Within a Reasonable Time

This next set of articles actually has a few attached to it, not just one. It showcases the Jordan decision and its effect on cases and people.

The General Principal is:

The right to a trial within a reasonable time is guaranteed by s. 7 and 11(b) of the Charter.

Charter Right to Reasonable Time to Trial

Section 11(b) of the Canadian Charter entitles any "person charged with an offence ... the right ... to be tried within a reasonable time". Where there is a breach of this right, the available remedy to a court is a stay of proceedings.

In 2016, the Supreme Court of Canada re-framed the analysis for by setting presumptive ceilings of 18 and 30 months depending on defence election. The new "Jordan" analysis removed from consideration the prejudice to the accused and the seriousness of the offence.

Section 11(b) protects three individual rights:

• the accused's right to security of person by minimizing the anxiety and stigma of criminal proceedings;

• the accused's right to liberty by minimizing the effect of pre-trial custody or restrictive bail conditions; and

• the accused's right to a fair trial by ensuring that the proceedings occur while evidence is fresh and available.

It also protects societal rights:

• the public's interest in having our laws enforced by having those who break the law tried quickly; and

• the public's interest in having those accused of crime dealt with fairly.

Timely trials also affect societal interests by benefiting victims and witnesses, and instills public confidence in the administration of justice.

Jordan Framework

The new framework is designed in part to "do away with prejudice as an express factor in assessing delay". It was considered "confusing, hard to prove, and highly subjective". It does not, however, ignore the existence of prejudice, it simply creates a legal presumption of prejudice once the ceiling has been breached.

The reason also for the change was to address the "culture of complacency" among Crown, defence and courts that have developed in modern years. This culture is exhibited in delay causing conduct, including:

- unnecessary procedures;
- unnecessary adjournments;
- inefficient practices by all parties; and
- inadequate institutional resources.

The message from Jordan is that "all participants in the system are to take proactive measures at all stages of the trial process to move cases forward and bring accused persons to trial in a timely fashion."

Judges are charged with curtailing delay and changing courtroom culture. Practices causing delay that were once tolerated are no longer permitted. This can include denying defence adjournments where it could result in unacceptably long delays despite it being time attributable to defence.

Basically, it's the court trying to get cases moving at a reasonable pace. It is 18 Months for Provincial courts and 30 Months for Superior Court. If a trial hasn't been heard or tried by then, it can be stayed or thrown out.

It was controversial as we were seeing many people that were guilty having their charges stayed, or getting away with crime. Same thing as I'm talking about employee fraud, but there were real cases of murder, and the people went free because the court was taking too long. I won't comment because it is much harder to swallow and I feel bad for the families.

JORDAN (11B) CHARTER

In July 2016, the Supreme Court of Canada placed another big limitation on the ability of fraud victims to obtain justice through the Canadian criminal justice system with the release of the decision of R. v. Jordan.

In R. v. Jordan, the Supreme Court of Canada put restrictions on the opportunity to have criminal cases adjudicated on the merits by declaring that a criminal case must be heard within an arbitrary time limit or the case will be stayed by reason of infringing an the accused's section 11(b) Charter right to have a trial within a "reasonable time". Most fraud victims are of the view that if their criminal complaint is not adjudicated on the merits, and if a restitution order is not issued, there is no justice.

In the Jordan case, the majority of the judges of the Supreme Court of Canada put the Charter rights of an accused ahead of the rights of victims, bringing into question whether the justice being issued is really "reasonable". A brief legal analysis of the R. v. Jordan case follows below, but to understand the implications of the decision, fraud victims should review the following press releases:

HUNDREDS OF FINANCIAL CRIME PROSECUTIONS COULD BE STAYED, SENATOR SAYS

Published by Dan Fumano on September 20, 2016,

Charles Kamal Dass, who was a registered investment adviser in Port Alberni, was charged with 15 counts of theft, fraud, and forgery, based on transactions with 13 individuals and two corporations between 2000 and 2007, the court heard.

All charges have now been stayed because of what a judge called an unreasonably long wait for a trial. No allegations were proven in court. One of the complainants, George Haack, said that the staying of criminal charges had shaken his faith in the justice system. Canadian Senator George Baker, Deputy Chair of the Standing Senate Committee on Legal and Constitutional Affairs, said: "You'll note now that every judge who throws a case out highlights the 'culture of complacency.'" Fraud cases could be among the most likely cases to be dropped, Baker said, along with drug-trafficking cases, due to the complex nature of such investigations, including many search warrants and forensic analysis. Baker said: "These are complicated cases that take long periods of time and if you have a culture of complacency in the courts–which we do have, according to every judge, every court. If this complacency doesn't disappear, then it's going to be a great time for criminals because they'll just be released because time will have run out." Asked to estimate the number of financial fraud cases that could be stayed after the Jordan decision, Baker said: "There could be hundreds."

THE JORDAN DECISION

The decision of the Supreme Court of Canada in R. v. Jordan was split from 5 to 4. Four of the judges hearing the Jordan case disagreed with what the other five judges decided was a "reasonable" right for an accused relating to the time to get to trial. As most fraud victims will note, for every right adjudicated in the favour of an accused, there is a corresponding infringement on the right of a victim to have his or her complaint tested on the merits. To better understand this infringement, we review what the minority (the four judges who disagreed with the other five), had to say about what is "reasonable". The headnote summarized their position in part as:

The majority's new framework is not an appropriate approach to interpreting and applying the s. 11 (b) right, for several reasons. First, the new approach reduces reasonableness to numerical ceilings. Reasonableness cannot be judicially defined with precision or captured by a number. The majority's approach also exceeds the proper role of the Court. Creating fixed or presumptive ceilings is a task better left to legislatures. The ceilings place new limits on the exercise of the s. 11(b) right to a trial within a reasonable time for reasons of administrative efficiency that have nothing to do with whether the delay in a given case was or was not excessive. This is inconsistent with the judicial role. The majority's approach also risks negative consequences for the administration of justice. The presumptive ceilings are unlikely to improve the pace at which the vast majority of cases move through the system. As well, if this new framework were applied immediately, the majority's transitional provisions will not avoid the risk of thousands of judicial stays. Moreover, the increased simplicity which is said to flow from the majority's new framework is likely illusory. Even if creating ceilings were an appropriate task for the courts and even if there were an appropriate evidentiary basis for them, there is little reason to think these ceilings would avoid the complexities inherent in deciding whether a particular delay is unreasonable. The majority's framework simply moves the complexities of the analysis to a new location: deciding whether to rebut the presumption that a delay is unreasonable if it exceeds the ceiling in particular cases. Ultimately, the majority's new framework casts aside three decades of the Court's jurisprudence when no participant in the appeal called for such a wholesale change has not been the subject of adversarial scrutiny or debate, and risks thousands of judicial stays. In short, the new framework is wrong in principle and unwise in practice.

FRAUD TRIAL DELAYS: EX-SECURITY AGENCY OWNER LUIGI CORETTIE WON'T BE TRIED

Superior Court Judge France Charbonneau released businessman Luigi Coretti from all charges after the Crown issued a request for a stay of proceedings. Coretti faced charges of fraud and forgery in connection with the accounting operations of his security agency, BCIA. The charges dated back to 2012. His lawyer filed a motion to stay the proceedings on the heels of the Supreme Court of Canada's Jordan decision. The trial was scheduled to take place in 2018, six years after Coretti was arrested. He had been at the heart of corruption news when he was alleged to have loaned a credit card to former minister Tony Tomassi, who used it for personal reasons. Tomassi pleaded guilty in 2011 to a charge of fraud in this case. He used the card for gasoline, even though he had a travelling allowance as an elected member of the National Assembly. The charges against Coretti were not tested in court.

FRAUD VICTIMS SHOULD NOT RELY ON THE CRIMINAL JUSTICE SYSTEM FOR RECOVERY

In an article entitled "Man Defrauds Own Family, Friends", the story is told of how fraudster Michael Di Giulio took millions from his own family. In response to frustration with the criminal process, one of the victims was quoted as saying: "Quite frankly, I really don't care what they do to him and how they deal with him. I need my money back. I want my money back." Ultimately this is where we find most fraud victims end up. While many fraud victims initially want the fraudster to be punished, they come to realize that the criminal justice system is a high-stakes game – where Judges (who are funded by taxpayers), complain about the government-run Courts and Crown prosecutors (who are also funded by the public) as living in a culture of complacency, while fraud victims see the government and the Courts living in a culture focused on the Charter rights of the accused as if they are some holy grail at the expense of their own rights to justice. To state otherwise, while the Courts cloak themselves in the comfort that the Charter is the ultimate law in the country, this does not resonate well with victims who have no "right" they can point to in the Charter to ensure their criminal complaint is fairly dealt with on the merits. It is because of decisions like Jordan that fraud victims ultimately give up on pursuing justice through the criminal system. It is because the criminal process is risky at best that fraud victims should protect their own interests and pursue justice and restitution by first suing the fraudster and their accomplices in the civil court system where Charter rights do not exist.

Source: canadianfraudnews.com, and investigationcounsel.com

WHAT FRAUD VICTIMS SHOULD KNOW ABOUT CRIMINAL SENTENCING- AN UPDATE ON PROBLEMS WITH RELYING ON CRIMINAL RESTITUTION ORDERS.

On July 28, 2015, investment fraudsters Garry Sorenson and Milowe Brost were sentenced in their criminal trial to 12 years in jail. The Reasons for Judgment were just released by the Court, which is what prompted this blog post. The Court declared the fraud perpetrated by Sorenson and Brost to be the "biggest fraud in Canadian history" involving potentially $200M and potentially 850 victims. Despite the magnitude of this fraud, the Court did not impose the maximum sentence of 14 years in prison or make restitution or fine-in-lieu-of-forfeiture order. Remarkably, the Court held:

"The Criminal Court is ill-equipped to determine amounts to be payable to so many individuals [victims] in so many different circumstances. The amounts to be repaid are not readily ascertainable on the evidence before me. Accordingly, and with some regret, I leave the matter of recovery to the civil courts, and I decline to order restitution herein." We have written in the past about our concern for fraud victims who intend to rely on the criminal justice system as a means to recover their fraud loss. In the Sorenon and Brost case, many of the fraud victims did not file civil claims within the statutory limitation period and they are now statute-barred from bringing a civil fraud recovery case, as suggested by the criminal court. This decision–in Canada's largest investment fraud case–underscores why all fraud victims should engage civil fraud recovery counsel, if for no other reason than to preserve their right to recovery–even if the right is preserved until after the criminal process has run its course. The link to our prior blog post on Enforcing Criminal Restitution Orders and the Canadian Victims Bill of Rights. This more fully explains the law applying to criminal restitution orders. This post relies on the decision of Sorenson and Brost to provide information to fraud victims on other aspects of criminal sentencing in fraud cases, such as the importance of Victim Impact Statements and the purpose, from a criminal law perspective, of criminal sentencing. Victim Impact Statements

If a restitution order is not made by a Criminal Court, at least the victim will have an avenue (the civil system) through which to pursue recovery. As mentioned above, some of the victims in the Sorenson and Brost case no longer have a right to recovery because they mistakenly believed they could preserve their right to recovery through the criminal system.

I want to urge anyone who is in need of civil representation to reach out the team at investigativecounsel.com

Using a victim's money to defend a criminal prosecution

The below case highlights a law that allows the defendant to put a petition in to be able to access funds that have been frozen on them for court costs. So, what could happen?

The victim pays their civil counsel to get a freeze on some assets or cash and then the defence can claim they are broke, and be able to access those funds? In the end, if they lost the case, those funds would also be lost. So, the victim having access to the frozen funds as an argument is a non-event.

There is another decision used similar to this called Robotham. It allows the defendant to apply to the local municipalities and make them pay for the court costs. I will just leave it like that. My mother used to say, if you don't have anything nice to say …

Below is a statement from Norman Groot, a senior lawyer from the fraud recovery law firm Investigative Counsel PC

"Rogues can apply to a court to use a victim's money to defend a criminal prosecution–and Canada's *Charter of Rights* does not assist victims of fraud–only the cons," Groot said. "There is no limitation period on filing a criminal complaint. There is no right to silence in the civil law system. We typically investigate to the point where the cops simply need to validate. This often assists the police, as a significant problem in the criminal justice system is often referred to as "Jordan", where criminal prosecutions get stayed because it infringed some rogue's right to a speedy trial. Canada's *charter* litigation is imbalanced, and it does not give victims a right to a speedy recovery."

He said Canadian criminal restitution orders and criminal forfeiture orders are "more fiction than substance".

"Too often, Canadian criminal cases are dismissed for reasons having nothing to do with the victims," said Groot. "Even if the criminal system does result in a conviction and a restitution order is issued, the Canadian criminal system does not enforce it. A victim has to hire a civil lawyer to use to seek recovery."

He also said another issue for fraud victims to consider is that civil actions have to be commenced within two years from discovering the loss.

"Too often criminal cases take far longer than two years and then fail," he said. "If a civil case isn't started before the criminal case fails, the victim is left without any access to justice. Victims are better off to sue first, see if a recovery can be made, and then decide whether or not to file a criminal complaint."

ACKNOWLEDGEMENTS

The main contacts for any facts, statistics or fraud related news in this book come from 3 sources.

As mentioned, any statistic or report will come from ACFE. https://www.acfe.com/ Report to the Nations by the Association of Certified Fraud Examiners, Inc.

Any news, blog or current info comes from canadianfraudnews.com/ and investigationcounsel.com

Early on in my research and readings I quickly became drawn to the integrity of the two sites mentioned above. The founder Norman Groot and his work as a fraud recovery litigator as well as a victim advocate in regards to fraud in Canada. He seems to shoot from the hip and always has the most up to date knowledge and information when it comes to Fraud laws in Canada. When i learned that they also work hand in hand with the ACFE it really didn't surprise me. I just wished I had found them sooner. I urge anyone in need of counsel to engage with Norman and his team at investigationcounsel.com

Sources: 2020 *Report to the Nations*. Copyright 2020 by the Association of Certified Fraud Examiners, Inc.https://www.acfe.com/

Sources:canadianfraudnews.com/

Sources: www.investigationcounsel.com

by Norman Groot, LLB, CFE, CFI

Sources: www.investigationcounsel.com

by Dan Fumano on September 20, 2016, https://investigationcounsel.com/Services/legal-information-for-fraud-victmis-blogs-from-the-series-what-fraud-victims-should-know-about/

Sources: supremeadvocacy.ca sentencing-fine-in-lieu-of-forfeiture/

ALSO BY JOHN BALL

THE INTRUDER A book by John Ball

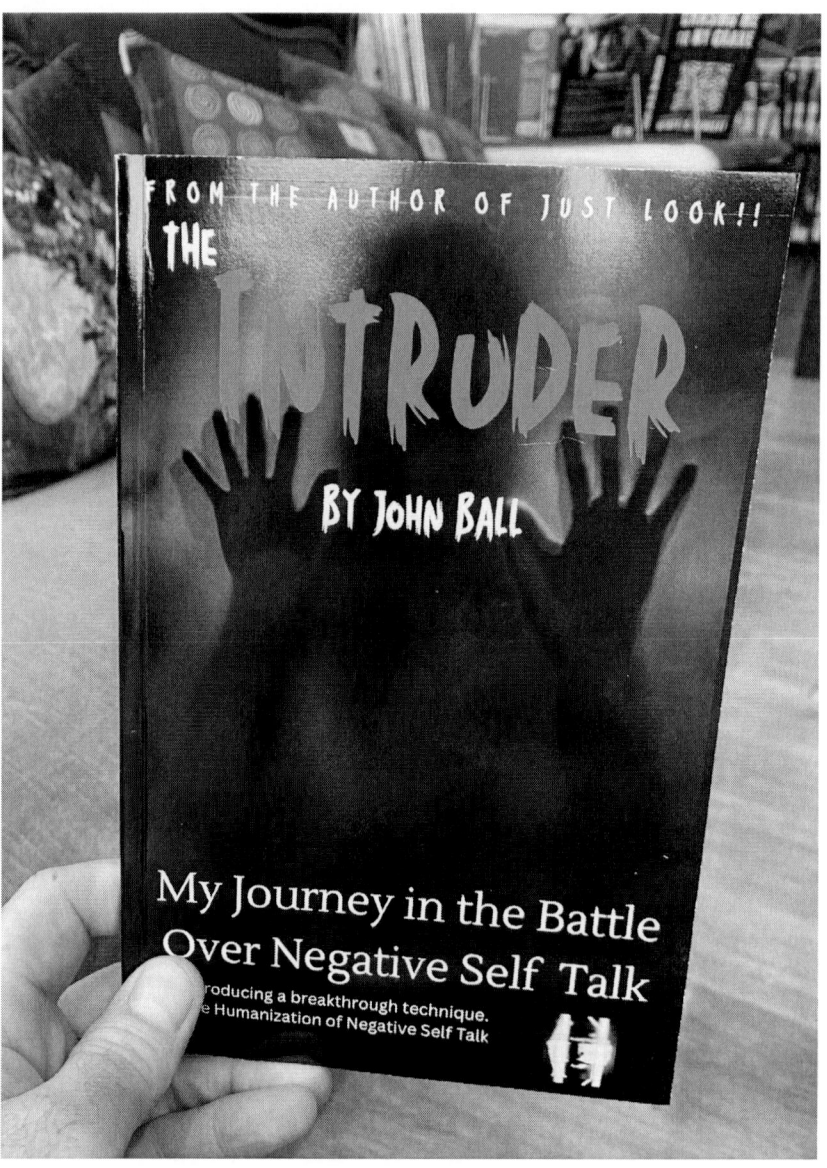

When the dust settled. I remember thinking to myself that after 10-12 years, I needed to finish what I started. I need to find the answer to eliminate Negative Self Talk. I owed it to myself and everyone else involved that was hurt by this. I thought "After all this time, I look around, having lost almost everything that we worked for. Thinking of the money that was stolen, the money that we had spent on civil legal fees, the once thriving business itself on life support, my marriage all but done, 10-12 years of my time and most, if not all of my confidence. The one thing that added insult to injury was after going through all of that and wasting all that time, the cruel joke was that the negative self talk was still there. So I gathered up all of the notes and research that was sitting for 12 years and promised myself one thing. After this weekend. I will find the answer One way or another.... I'm taking the notes and research into a room and locking the door. I promised myself, Only one of us is coming out of this room after the weekend is over. Either I walk out or the Intruder does.....

Excerpt From THE INTRUDER: MY JOURNEY IN THE BATTLE OVER NEGATIVE SELF TALK John Ball THE INTRUDER was created while John was searching for unrelated files at the end of writing his first book. He stumbled upon notes and research that was done years before on something that had been haunting him for some time. Negative mind talk or Mind chatter some call it. These notes turned into a presentation and similar companion book now called the INTRUDER. His journey into the battle against Negative self talk. How he thought something that had been said to him could make him stumble so bad that it effected his ability to lead, to run the company and even to sell. in the book, he goes down self admitted rabbit holes looking for answers to how negative mind talk begins. What is commonly done to treat it. Where does it come from?He even looks at old world and even ancient procedures. He looks at meditation, psychotherapy, pharmacological interventions, Buddhism and stress. He tries to bring forward anything that helps and leave behind anything else. In the end, he will showcase what could be a groundbreaking response to negative self talk. The Humanization of Negative Self Talk.

Product Details

Price

$14.19

Publisherv Lulu.com

Publish Date January 15, 2023

Pages 144

Dimensions 6.0 X 9.0 X 0.31 inches | 0.44 pounds

Language English

TypePaperback

EAN/UPC 9781365963063

BISAC Categories:

Diseases - Nervous System (incl. Brain)

Personal Growth - General

Mindfulness & Meditation

JOHN BALL

SPEAKER-AUTHOR

- www.linkedin.com/injohn-ball-05a8683b
- john@johnball.ca
- +548-882-9220
- www.johnball.ca

JOHN BALL
SPEAKER-AUTHOR-
MOTIVATOR

MEET JOHN BALL

C.E.O of a Media Corporation for over 25 yrs #16 on Profit Magazines 100 fastest growing companies.
Featured in the Globe and Mail-Tips from the top and countless magazines and news outlets. Author of Just Look and The Intruder

JUST LOOK!! is based on Johns first hand experience relating to employee based fraud. He spent the better part of 12 years, after his company fell victim to a large scale, employee based fraud. In and out of court rooms, Crown, attorneys and Civil lawyers offices alike. Being involved in a case like this specifically gave him insight into the system, changes that need to happen to the system but won't and how the victims in these situations can feel helpless and victimized again and again.

His goal is to help someone out there someone who doesn't know it's happened to them yet or someone who is just about to find out. If he can get to them soon enough, they don't have to go through what his company went through.

"If I can help one person not go through with any of us went through it's worth it I want to help business owners understand where the early detection signs and red flags are and We have an extensive checklist of procedures and actions anyone can put in place to mitigate and even eliminate fraud in their workplace."

THE INTRUDER was created while John was searching for unrelated files at the end of writing his first book. He stumbled upon notes and research that was done years before on something that had been haunting him for some time. Negative mind talk or Mindchatter some call it. These notes turned into a presentation and similar companion book now called the INTRUDER. His journey into the battle against Negative self talk. How he thought something that had been said to him could make him stumble so bad that it effected his ability to lead, to run the company and even to sell. in the book, he goes down self admitted rabbit holes looking for answers to how negative mind talk begins. What is commonly done to treat it. Where does it come from?He even looks at old world and even ancient procedures. He looks at meditation, psychotherapy, pharmacological interventions, Buddhism and stress. He tries to bring forward anything that helps and leave behind anything else. In the end, he will showcase what could be groundbreaking responses to negative self talk. The Humanization of Negative Self Talk and Interruptive sequencing.